THE VIEW FROM HERE

Unveiling The Tools of Self-Mastery
to Find, Accept and Love Oneself

Alexis Ajinça

The events and conversations in this book have been set down to the best of the author's ability, although some names and details have been changed to protect the privacy of individuals.

Copyright © Alexis Ajinça, 2021

Book Cover Design by: Chelsea Alphonso
Cover Photography by: Breonna Collier
A WritersBlok Production

Printed in the United States of America
First edition, 2021.
Hardcover ISBN 978-1-7369103-0-6
Ebook ISBN 978-1-7369103-1-3

DEDICATION

This book is dedicated to my mother; a woman who has incredible strength, work ethic and values. I wouldn't be the man I am today without her guidance. I am thankful to have her by my side in the absence of my father. I know he is watching over our family and I hope I have made him proud.

CONTENTS

INTRODUCTION

É tienne, like Saint-Étienne, France, is where I made my
first appearance in this world. Dubbed Charly, after my
great-grandfather. And Alexis, no fancy story here, it is simply
the name my parents both liked and agreed on. I grew up in a
good neighborhood, middle-class family, and loving home. My
mother, the Queen of The Kitchen, poured her heart into every
meal she served. My two older siblings, who have always and
to this day, complain that I am the favorite child - an undeniable
truth. And my father, an exteriorly tough guy with the ability
to touch a room through laughter. I take after him, serious but
witty. In school, I was an appreciated distraction from my classmates and held in wavering regard by my teachers. I have always had a passion for making the people around me feel good.
My wife will attest that I know just the right strings to pull,
when, and how hard. Enough to get right under her skin to get
on her nerves and the finesse required to reel her into a reluctant
smile and needed laugh. Transforming a rigid mood and breaking it down into something softer, was my first known talent.

I am no stand-up comedian but I understand the power that
laughter holds, and I know that it does everyone some good.
Reading tension and knowing when to break it up, has always
been a sixth sense of mine. The ability to shift the atmosphere
in a room is an art and a tool I have learned to employ at a very
young age. *Thanks, Dad.* What I have realized about laughter

is that it keeps me young. It is reviving. The pressures of the world are no joke. Life's hits and misses are inevitable. The situations that come our way, age us at a faster pace than what I believe is intended. With all of the mess around us, those few seconds reunite us with life's true purpose. It blesses us with perspective and corrects our lens, and even if, for a moment, it's worth every second. Laughter can peel back the layers of defense we've built up along life's way. It disarms us. It allows us to be vulnerable. It forces us to drop the weights, relax, and release. To be just as we were as a child: innocent, free, fun, and with a deep capacity to love. Those features that make us the beings we were created to be are often stripped away and replaced with worry, doubt, and fear. We forget the freedom of just being who we are as we are. We rid times of play and creativity and drown our spirits in stressed competition - the rat race that never ends. All so that our love, once unconditional, takes up less and less space. I strongly believe that we need to actively create the space for love and laughter to reclaim their rightful place. That place is where we feel safe and loved. That place saves lives.

The momentary relief laughter provides is not only healing but an essential means to our graceful survival. We need those breaks. Growing up, my home provided that safe place. It was that light atmosphere that made life on the outside that much easier. I have done my best to bring that spirit into my home today. I still try to infuse it into my relationships. Those who know me know that sooner or later, in my presence, they will ease into a smile, and if they aren't playing hard to get, maybe crack a laugh. This is one way that I contribute. A small effort, a small gesture, a priceless impact.

While my childhood progressed at an expected pace, my body quickly advanced. By fourteen years old, I grew past my two older siblings and parents to become the tallest person in the home. When I was fifteen, my size 16 feet unwillingly dangled off the bottom of my bed. Since fourteen, I have easily been able to survey the top of every head in the room. Sitting brings many up to my eye level, but in most cases, my neck awkwardly arches downward to help me make eye contact with those below me. I have grown to a towering height of 7'2" tall. To put that into perspective, I can not walk through a standard door frame without ducking to compensate for an additional 6". Even if it looks like I can make it, ducking is a non-negotiable custom. I have hit my head too many times to take the chance. I can not walk into a store and effortlessly buy shoes for my size eighteen feet. I can't just sit in any vehicle, I simply do not fit. And driving? The selection is narrow. Few cars have the specs to accommodate mine.

Being tall does have its advantages. For starters, there is a lot more of me to love. This is crucial to my survival at home because I tend to get on my wife's nerves... a lot. My height also gave me the edge I needed in my basketball career. In 2008 my life changed when I was drafted to the NBA by the Charlotte Bobcats. They say that tall people tend to be healthier, happier, and more productive. Apparently, tall people are even more successful. They also say that tall people are seen as more confident. And while all of that may be true, perception is not always reality. The truth is, I have struggled with self-confidence since I was a child. After years of teasing and impolite stares, I grew to not like the man I saw in the mirror. As I continue on my journey of self-work, I spend a lot of time making sense of myself and my unique idiosyncrasies. Who I am and what makes me, me. I want to know why I've made certain choices and decisions and I want to understand what circumstances have informed the man I am today. Why has laughter always been a pillar in my life? While I understand laughter is a gift, I now know that it has also been my way of avoiding internal conflict in response to my harsh external environment. At times, laughter may have been used to ease my discomfort and divert attention away from my insecurities. Laughter has been my mask.

Being tall has been a blessing, but it has also been the root of my struggles and the pit of many of my lows. Being tall means I'm the first seen in a room. It means that people look up to me, not just because they have to, but because they expect I have the answer. I do not have room to hide. I can never be discreet. I have to be that much stronger physically and mentally to match my dominant physique. I can never go unnoticed in public. I am always within someone's view. And when you don't have the confidence to stick out, being tall can be utterly uncomfortable. Tall, skinny legs and noticeably large feet were features I desperately wanted to erase. Since I looked different, I felt different; and once people began to treat me differently, I started to do the same. My need to feel normal caused my identity to suffer. I lost myself. My esteem plummeted, and the tall-successful-confident-man the world saw was only a shell of those features. Now that I've made the commitment to the process and reflect on my 'why's', I am gaining control over my mind and my responses. It's not only my responsibility to make others around me feel good, but it is my vow to afford myself the same pleasures. Every day the work continues. I am in a constant season of growth. I know that my insecurities and anxieties have a purpose and through my story, I want to be a voice of hope and inspiration for others.

Being different is inevitable - no two people are identical. Feeling different, on the other hand, can either work against you or for you. If you have felt different in ways that reduce your self-worth... If you struggle with finding yourself, accepting yourself, and being yourself... If you are familiar with the pain endured from being on the outside... This book is for you. I aim to help you find the power within yourself to start your journey. Through my story, my goal is to push you to reflect on your being, pull out the tools we were all given, and utilize them to become the best version of you: the strong, confident, courageous, boldly happy - you.

Find you, accept you, be you.

- Alexis

PART I.
ON THE BLACKTOP

CHAPTER 1

Growing Into The Other

Below The Field

Not so much a sight today, but my childhood street was always busy and buzzed with the sounds of children at play. As soon as I got the okay from mom, I joined the rest of the kids on my street; going home only to eat, use the bathroom, and always before the streetlights came on. We lived in a middle-class suburb in a cul-de-sac of Saint-Étienne, France. All of us went to the same elementary school, and every evening we claimed the street as our own. The cars that came in knew the drill and worked their way around us. As soon as my homework was done (to my parents' standards), I jumped house-to-house rounding up the troops; and if I had already been summoned, it was a dash for the front door with the hope that I didn't miss out on any action. You never wanted to be the kid that missed something good. For my siblings and me, our neighborhood and the home was our haven. It was safe. Trusting and predictable. Light and fun.

Above the field, was different. There was nothing safe or predictable about it. You had to watch your back. Only a few blocks away the sounds of soccer and tag were drowned out by noise. The kind of noise that made you more resilient than you should have to be as a child. The kind of noise that we were warned to stay far away from. The school is what brought the two neighborhoods together, and the field is what kept us apart. Despite our common grounds on school property, my father never let us play outside of the cul-de-sac. Doing his best to protect us as long as he possibly could, above the field was forbidden territory. He knew the looser his grip the more opportunity to step into the hands of life's harmful unpleasantries. Below the field is where we stayed.

A police officer, my dad ran a tight ship but always from a place of love. Stern but always had time for a joke. Serious but soft. When he spoke we listened. We grew up with a solid fear of disappointing him; and until we developed our moral compasses, that fear was great enough to keep us well within our respective lanes. My mother, a social worker, naturally beamed as a nurturer. She kept the house in top shape and filled it with love. Together, they balanced each other quite well. I am the youngest of three. Separated by ten years from my brother and eight years from my sister, the gap made it difficult to share similar interests at times, but fortunately, our bond never suffered. We were tight. Those two have always had my back without hesitation. They taught me what true loyalty and support mean.

Comparable to the family dynamic in many homes, our birth order influenced our upbringing. By the time my parents were tasked with raising me, they were slightly burnt out. My brother had little to no freedom. As the first and only girl child, my sister had less than him. Then there was me. I had it far laxer. The grip eased, and I got away with much more than my siblings did. Having realized the shifted dynamic, I took advantage and enjoyed every bit of added leniency that the order afforded me. Still far from loose, but not as strict as when my parents were new to the game. I vividly recall the explosion that erupted from my dad's body when he discovered my brother, Guillaume's tattoo. I'm sure my dad saw red. My brother and I laugh about it now, but back then, I was afraid for Guillaume. My dad fumed for what felt like months and we were all sure to not poke the bear. The floors of our home became thin as ice, and we tip-toed around accordingly. Every irritant, related or not, made the incident fresh again and set dad off as if he was seeing the tattoo for the first time. All of that drama, all of that yelling, all of those threats, only to not react when I came home in a similar fashion several years later. The favorite child by far, though my mom will never admit it. She treated me like a baby and I let her. My siblings poked at how big our kisses were and how tight she hugged me. I would envy me too.

When I was five years old, I decided to follow in my sibling's footsteps and began BMX racing. I loved how widely fun and competitive it was. There was a constant adrenaline rush and pursuit of speed. After some time, I had caught up to my brother's skill level and was quite good. The World Championships were being held in Saskatoon, Canada, and both my brother and I had qualified. A far ways away from Saint-Ètienne, but the travel was not a barrier. Not only was it far, but it was very costly. My parents were not in a position to cover the fare for the entire family to attend, so they agreed on sending the three of us to Canada. Of course, under strict warning and guidelines. Guillaume didn't make it past the first round but I did. Despite his early elimination, he opted to video record my next few races. I love watching them to this day. Not to see myself race, but to hear Guillaume roaring in support and cheering me on. He has always been in my corner, pushing me to do better and be better.

Together we were a unit. Bonded and strong. We supported and loved one another the way a family should. In our home, we were taught to be expressive. To not shy away from sharing our feelings. To be okay with feeling emotional and being vulnerable. Our nights ended with a kiss from mom and an 'I love you' from dad. My dad did shift work but always chose to work nights so that during the day, he could pick me up for lunch and cook something for us at home. All the way up until grade five, we spent every lunch eating and watching TV. As a family, we kept up with holiday traditions and had many of our own. More often than not, my dad's extensive vinyl collection beat through the hallways. Michael Jackson was his album of choice and we all knew every word. At Christmas, my mom appeased each one of us and cooked our favorite meals. Duck, liver, oysters, and lobster filled the dining room table every year. She showed her love through food and stands as the best chef I know to date. As the youngest, it was a tradition for me to give my gifts to the elders first before opening my own. Despised then, but I understand it's the purpose now.

Born in Guadeloupe, a French island in the West Indies, my dad came to France by himself. We would all make the trip every couple of years in the summer to see his side of the family. I remember those trips as some of my favorite memories together. Those vacations allowed us to spend the most time with one another. Unbothered, uninterrupted by work, school, and the hustle of back home. The water was crystal clear, perfect for snorkeling. There my sister taught me how to drive. She was eighteen, I had just turned ten, and she let me sit behind the wheel on the way to the beach where the road was usually empty. The car had manual gears and we doubled over laughing every time I stalled.

All of these memories made home, a home; and family my rock. My parents did an amazing job of raising my brother, sister, and me. They were protective, hard but reasonable, and above all, loving. My family was the single most important influence when I was growing up and steady support into adulthood. They weren't about looking good and putting on a show. They were about raising good people, with strong values, and offering solid examples of how to live accordingly. I know my nature to be kind is because they showered me with kindness. I am almost certain my expression of love grew to be healthy in part due to observing what real love looks like.

We didn't have it all, but we had each other; and for me, that was more than enough. As a family we were good. As an individual, battling the complexities of life became challenging. Somewhere between home (my foundation) and the outside (the noise), I lost sight of who I was. I struggled to accept myself despite what I was taught and believed to be true. When I gave access to the outside to dictate who I was on the inside, it altered my esteem. My confidence faltered, and my once deeply rooted identity became extinct. The more of the outside that I let in, the more of myself I gave up. Listening to the opinions of others and offering them a place to fester was cancerous. Their words began to metastasize with no remedy to slow its growth. Ruminating thoughts replaced my once sound mind, and I became accustomed to sacrificing my peace to make room for lies that didn't belong. I no longer fit because I was trying to fit a mold that wasn't mine. I accept that somewhere between home and the outside, I lost myself in a place where my family could not find nor save me. It was up to me to find my way back home.

Letting The Outside In

I became acquainted with the challenges that came along with being Black at seven years old. It was the last day of summer camp, and on that day we would always have a party. Dancing, food, games, and goodbyes until the following year. My friends had hyped me up to approach a girl who I thought was cute. I gathered my nerves and went over to ask her to dance. All eyes were on me from across the floor. She barely looked up and said *no*. Not taking no without reason, I asked her why, to which she replied, "Because you're Black." I returned to my group of friends telling them that she said no and nothing more. At the moment I didn't process her words. I didn't know how to respond or feel. I enjoyed the rest of the evening on the surface but replayed her words until I fell asleep. This was the very first time I remember realizing my skin was Black. And Black not only implied difference but in some eyes meant unequal and unworthy. If I had to pinpoint the moment I knew I was different, this was it. Since that day, I started to pay attention too. I picked up on fairness and the lack thereof. I understood bias and discrimination before I ever knew the words existed. There were parts of me that made it hard for people to accept and like. Despite my kind nature or friendly disposition, what they saw was most important, and what they say they used to define me despite how I saw myself.

At eight years old, I had won a BMX championship. Not only did I win, but I destroyed my competition by a long stretch. My dad was so proud of me and that topped the achievement itself. One of the parents whose son was in the race was livid and reported me to the officials stating that we had lied about my age. The inaccurate assumption came from my tall stature. They demanded to see my birth certificate and my dad refused. Remaining calm as the day, he made sure to shift the blame to its rightful owner. It wasn't our fault that I was tall, it was their fault their son was short and beyond that a sore loser. After that experience, my height accompanied my race as one more feature vulnerable to my dissection. Again, I started to pay attention too. I noticed I was taller than all of my friends. I looked back on school pictures and in every class shot, I was the one standing in the back, off the bleachers, on the side, and right next to the teachers who I was quickly gaining on each year. By grade six I was 6'2" and not even the teachers looked down on me.

I grew faster than most. In fact, I grew faster than everyone around me. Past my classmates, past my parents, then my siblings, and I didn't stop there. Hand-me downs were good enough until Guillaume's old pants stopped brushing the ground and the floods continued to rise. My parents couldn't keep up. Financially, I knew they couldn't afford to replace my clothes at the same pace I was outgrowing them. Everything was too short. Beyond money, sourcing clothes that fit became the next issue. We simply could not find things that were proportionate to my limbs and when they did, it was a toss-up between pants that fit and pants that looked like they belonged to a seventy-five-year-old man. When a new style would come out, every kid would beg for a trip to the store. For me, those trips slowly stopped, and that excitement quickly died. Just when I had lost all hope, the high sock trend was born! Heaven sent! This was the one style that served me and well. I was able to pull up my socks over my sweatpants and hide the two sometimes three-inch gap to my shoes. I caught onto this trend very quickly and gave it life long after it died.

Keeping up with the rest of my body, I outgrew sizes every few months. There was never an opportunity to own a shoe collection much less have more than one pair. Nike Air Max Sharks - those were the ones! They started to pop up on every foot around me. Every day another one of my friends got them. By this time, I was already a size fourteen and couldn't locate my size anywhere. Even if my parents could afford them, I couldn't find them. I quickly realized my friends and I were not going to share the same styles. I got what fit and what was in the budget. Nothing more. The bigger my body grew, the more money was spent trying to keep up. Although my feet outgrew my shoes, I wore them for the better part of a year. I did everything in them from recess to soccer. As a result, my shoes were challenged with keeping up as well. Holes took over the bottom soles. If it rained, my feet were never dry. And seeing how hard my parents worked, I knew to never ask for more than what they gave me. So while my feet pushed the inner limits of my shoes and began to hurt, I waited until they gifted me with a new pair each time. My parents were not new to these challenges. At 6'7" and ten years before my time, Guillaume's options were much less. For Elodie, who is 5'11" and size forty-one in shoes, the struggle continued and heightened when trying to find appropriate apparel for females.

As I stretched out, my thin physique became more noticeable. Not only was I extremely tall, but I was skinny. Very skinny. I used to hate wearing shorts because they showed my legs. *French baguette* (a long thin loaf of bread). That's what the school kids would call me. Referring to my legs of course. They teased me, warning me not to jump too high to avoid snapping them on my way down. There are no better words to describe how I felt, other than hate. I hated it. I hated my legs. I hated how skinny they were and how tall I was. Guillaume had once bought me a pair of jean shorts that were really nice and most importantly, fit. They had the Cleveland Cavaliers team logo on the back, exactly what was in style at the time. I didn't want to seem ungrateful, but after a week or so of not wearing them, he asked why. I had to tell him I couldn't wear the shorts because I would only be setting myself up to be looked at awkwardly and teased. He reassured me to not worry. And he reminded me that when he was picked on, he overcame it through learning how to love himself. Once he was able to do that, all the noise on the outside was silenced. His words meant enough for me to at least try, and I did. I trusted him and took his advice to heart. I tried to find the strength to begin the journey of self-love and maybe through my next steps, it was a start. I began wearing the shorts he bought for me and others that got a push to the back of my drawers. Slowly my comfort level increased.

Despite my efforts, the more I tried to embrace who I was, the more I was attacked. The bits of confidence I would muster up were expended defending myself. By the fifth grade, it escalated from verbal to physical attacks. The fights were constant, and I became very accustomed to defending myself. I was easily triggered and always in defense mode. The lightest poke would set me off. Fighting became my new norm. Whenever Elodie caught wind of something going on, she always came to my rescue. She was often bigger than the kids I was up against, and she gracefully took them out one by one. Her punches came in heavy and fast. Even our dog, Orky, a German Shepherd joined the squad. He once saw Elodie fighting and jumped the fence and gate to get his paws on a guy. We were a team. After every battle, we walked away heads up and tall. The way my family stuck up for me, is where I learned to stick up for others. At school, if my friends were getting picked on, I used my words first and my fists second. Their fight was my fight. After continued office calls and suspensions, my parents had enough. I was withdrawn from the school on the field with hopes I would have a fresh start somewhere else.

Your Pillar Is A Priority

My dad's advice never changed, "Love yourself." That was the morale of every story and the heart of every situation. It's what many lacked and avoided. According to him, it's what the world was deficient in. It was the root cause of all of the chaos and hate that consumed so many hearts. He would always do a double-take in the mirror and tell himself how handsome he was. He showed us what it looked like. He instructed us to practice it. He taught us that love on its own wasn't good enough; self-love must and always come first.

I knew how to love others. I was a giver. I was kind. I ran to the defense of many. What I missed, was the very thing my dad preached, self-love. I was never able to drown the noise that infiltrated my spirit. So, when I needed to pull from that center for stability and strength, there was nothing there. It was hard but I remember trying to emulate him. I remember standing, reciting his words to myself, and feeling nothing.

He was well aware of the challenges I faced, and when present, he too came to my defense. There were several times he consoled me when I was being attacked for things I couldn't help. My height, the color of my skin, my shoe size, and thin stature. "Don't let them see you cry son, don't let them know they got to you." He encouraged me to show emotion but never to the ones that caused the harm - my enemies. Instead, I was told to let it all out with family. Family is who he said I could trust to not take advantage of my vulnerability. He preached that true self-love births happiness. To be at peace with the chaos on the outside, I would have to accept who I was, and the skin I was in. Then, the noise wouldn't matter. Then, what people thought about me would make no difference. I was never able to get to that place he spoke of. I used to cry to my mom and ask her why I had to be so tall, so different. She told me that it's beautiful to be tall and different from the rest. Her words were comforting and tied me over to the next day, sometimes more, but I struggled to embed them any deeper to make them last any longer.

Both encouraged me to do anything I wanted, from swimming to judo, BMX, and eventually basketball. My dad was hard to impress. So when he told me he was proud of me, it meant the world. After winning a BMX Championship against the best in France, my mom radiated in pride. My dad told me I did a good job but the race was too close. He always pushed me to my limit and then some. My mom's smiles were nice to see and her hugs, nothing like them. But even just a good job from the big guy was no match in comparison. I intensely competed with a fear of disappointing him.

As far as the discipline in my home, my dad came down heavy. Whether it was for fighting, or not doing my homework, he always seemed to be there, waiting and ready to straighten me out. I once told him the word *no*. Boy, did I mess up! After the third time, he asked me to finish my homework he went for the belt. My mom was furious with him because of how hard he hit me. Not long after, the tough, soft guy apologized. It never changed my love for him, but right then and there I knew, no was never an option. Only a few weeks later, my friends and I had the bright idea of setting off fireworks in the school parking lot. The one I set off went too close to a man and his daughter getting in their car. The dad went to the principal. The principal went to my dad. And my dad's previous apology became water under the bridge, in addition to a two-day suspension. Extreme for some, but his discipline instilled my respect for authority and my awareness of boundaries. Hated it then, but love it now.

Between the two of them, the sacrifices made were immeasurable. Mom worked full days Monday to Friday, cooked every evening, cleaned every night, got us ready for the next day - not to mention weekends full of competitions - and did it all over again. Her husband was well taken care of. Her meals were from scratch. Sauces, bread, and spreads all whipped up with love. Dad was on nights, just to see us off in the mornings, spend time over the lunch break, and watch us walk home from school in the afternoons. I could tell they were both tired, but they somehow seemed to find the strength to do it again and again. We saved by taking the transit and went back home instead of staying overnight in hotels for competitions. We drove thirteen hours to the Czech Republic for the weekend because the airfare was too expensive, while the other families flew. Then back to work and school on Monday.

We all have pillars that serve as a foundation for our growth. Our mothers, fathers, loved ones, and experiences build on their strength. I had strong pillars. My family gave me the love and support I needed. Extrinsically, I was fed. Relying on their investments, I ignored my own. I took the encouragement and compassion they offered me, and it stopped there. Eventually, the power of their words and love fizzled out. Those pillars were not strong enough to stand on their own. Alone, they were not sustainable. I didn't invest in the most important pillar, my own. I was able to accept encouragement but didn't know how to encourage myself. I was loved but didn't know how to love myself. I was kind to others but treated myself with such disdain and hostility. There was no investment from me to me. My pillar needed love too.

Understanding The Power of Difference

I felt different because I was different. I know now there was nothing wrong with that because different is what we all are. There is absolutely nothing wrong with feeling or being set apart from the rest. Not one of us is identical. The problem, however, existed in my understanding of difference. The world has an evil way of tricking you into believing that being different means you are the minority. And how being a part of the minority means you are humanly less than everyone else. To not live as the majority brought lies of inferiority and self-doubt. It forced me to focus on difference as a problem and a complication rather than an advantage.

I struggled with my difference. Despite the love I received and despite the tools I was given, I wasn't able to find that intrinsic effort to love myself first. It didn't matter how much they said they loved me or how much love I gave them in return. It wasn't enough. My pillar was non-existent. My negative association with difference caused me to suffer silently. I hated the way I looked. I asked God why. I desperately wanted to fit in. I wanted to be able to hide. I wanted to remove the features that made me stand out. I didn't want to deal with any more height shaming or tall jokes and no more laughing or teasing, name-calling, or age debates. I wanted to go out and not feel the eyes of others scanning my body and analyzing my height. The more I paid attention to everyone else's reaction and response, the more I fed my insecurity. It grew with every word, and with each encounter, my confidence and self-esteem shriveled. Ironically, those were the only small things about me.

I had to learn how to compensate for the negative connotations people unfairly associated me with as a result of my height. I realized because I was so tall, I could easily be perceived as intimidating. When I walked in the opposite direction of others, they afforded me more space as they passed than what was socially required. In a line, they often stepped up to widen the gap between us, as if it would give room to my height. Looking down, as I always do, is known to change the perception of a facial expression. The same expression was seen from a lower perspective often alluded to a scowl that would have never existed if at an even height. So, I made sure to smile. Smile when I walked into a room when I greeted others, and when I cashed out at the store. Smiling seemed to break the illusion of intimidation that followed me. I became a great actor and used the parts of me that seemed to fit, to distract from my deemed dysfunction. I also came to understand that as a tall Black man, I was even more threatening.

They couldn't help themselves but stare. Even when they tried, they always managed to sneak a peek and I always caught them. Sometimes I had the energy to meet their eyes with mine and make them feel equally awkward. But most times, I was just aware. I began to obsess over all of these behaviors and non-verbal cues. I studied how people interacted with my tallness and Blackness and everything else that made me different. It was a never-ending social study. Even though I rarely responded,

I was actively waiting for someone to notice me and someone always did. Mind-torture, at its best.

The older I grew, the more time I spent away from my home and the more I had to face the cruelties of the outside. The more I grew in disdain of public settings. Socially I withdrew and only felt comfortable around those I knew - close family and friends and if I had it my way, I would always be at home. Being different hurt. It was tiring. I had to work hard at leveraging whatever I could find to belong. Emotionally I was drained. I needed a break. A day to not be seen or even a day to feel normal, but that was something I never received. I was stuck with me.

CHAPTER 2

Learning The Game

The Position That Moved Me

Our identity is often tied to what we do or who we are to others. A loose definition at best. A father, a teacher, or something to someone. To be clear, your identity is more than your job or your role. It's not a one-worded answer. In fact, the answer is quite complex and long-winded. Who you are is not what you do or what we often hear people define themselves as. It isn't a thing. Your identity consists of core internal tenets (influenced by external events), responsible for driving decisions that lead to the roles and positions we commonly associate with. It is more than a sum of your titles, it is the answer to all of your why's, why you love what, who you love, why you do what you do, why you've failed, why you're successful, why you reacted that way, and why you feel the way you do. When realized, it's the key to self-actualizing your potential, happiness, and inner peace. When ignored, we tend to adopt the identity of others and find ourselves lost and dissatisfied.

For some, the process of finding oneself can be triggered through these externalities. For myself, the catalyst was sports. For others, it can be anything from tragedy or simply the exhaustion acquired from living lost. I was introduced to basketball while

I was BMX racing. There weren't many players in my situation that I could look up to. I did, however, discover Jérôme Moïso. He was a French player who left his home to play in the NBA. At the time he was playing for the Toronto Raptors. Apart from his French roots, his family was also from the West Indies, like my father. I was motivated by our similar heritage and started to pay closer attention to the sport. Up until that point, I never had any attraction to the U.S. or desire to move there, but I knew that it would have to become a part of my story if I was going to get serious about ball.

I started playing when I was eleven years old. My cousin's husband made note of my height and suggested that I give it a try. So I squeezed basketball around my very tight BMX schedule. I started shooting around and hit the blacktop with the other kids. Starting basketball at eleven isn't late, but it certainly isn't early. Initially, my skill level was no match for the kids my age. I struggled to keep up. At first, I couldn't do anything, not even a simple layup! And of course, the other guys noticed and made it a point to let me know that I sucked. My only advantage was my height, and I used the hell out of it until my skills caught up. I remember my brother sitting me down and telling me I was going to have to make a choice: play for fun or play for more. Either way, he cautioned me to go in the direction that would make me most happy. He urged me to do what I love and in true Guillaume fashion, he reminded me that he would be there to support me either way. I decided to quit BMX racing and solely focus on basketball. And just like that, basketball took its place and became my number one.

Practices aggressively picked up and I worked tirelessly to get better. After a year of grinding, I was selected for the regional team. I still wasn't where I wanted or needed to be, but this was a step in the right direction. I needed to surround myself with the best in the region. Only a year in, I ended up with a bilateral knee injury. It started off as knee pain and quickly progressed. My doctor explained that it was a result of how fast I was growing - figures. I had worked my butt off, made the competitive team, and just like that the rest of the season was shot. With a brace on both knees, I sat on the bench during games and in practices. I worked on shooting from the unwanted comfort of a folding chair. The injury was my first major disappointment in sports. I had to get creative in mastering my craft if I wanted to succeed, so I made it a point to focus on what I had control over - my shot. My disappointment turned out to be a blessing in disguise. Two months of forced shooting made me really good. I was hitting nothing but net. Once I was cleared to go back on the court, I had something else to add to my resume other than a few more inches in height. I remember the coach stopping the team in the middle of practice, just to watch me shoot. It felt great!

The grind continued. I got better, much better. My handles improved. I was blocking shots. At sixteen my teammates would compare me to Kevin Garnett because we were both super tall and skinny, but most importantly, my game was on point. I found deep satisfaction in dunking on people. The rush and the reaction from the crowd were priceless, and I felt powerful. My dream of going to the league started to appear within reach. I professed it, and so did my teammates, who told me that I had to go. I continued to push myself and with that in mind, my focus narrowed even more. That was the goal and I made sure to position myself to get there. My dad knew very little about basketball. Correction, my dad knew nothing about basketball but being the father that he was, he made sure that changed. He wanted to be involved in my evolution and journey. That meant he had to pick up the game and fast. I fondly remember him taking the time to study the sport just so he could coach me. Basketball games and highlights took over the family TV. He picked it up quickly, and in return, he had a lot more to say about what I was and wasn't doing right.

I went to a French Academy for high school. Jessie, my best friend to this day, and I shared a room with two other guys - Ludovic and Olivier. For four years, we were in each other's faces morning till night and did everything together. My high school basketball coaches Richard and Philipe really helped groom me on and off the court. Richard was for me, and an advocate by any means. He pushed for me to make the team and stay on the team. When I first joined, they were unsure of which position I was going to play. Richard knew I could shoot so he made me play wing. The responsibility that came with this position was high, and so, he had to fight for me every year to hold my spot. From fourteen to seventeen years old, I was dubbed 'Too Long' on my high school team. My polar opposite, "Tip," was the shortest. For the first time being called something on account of my height didn't bother me, because I knew it came from a place of respect. For the first time, my height was working for me. This was the point in my life where my height and I made amends and started to get along. Of course, I still received

curious glares and unsolicited expressions, but I was less bothered. I found a way to use my difference for good. I put my
height to work and instead of fighting it, we started working
together. This is when I started my journey to self-acceptance.
It felt long overdue, but everything in time.

Basketball was tightly woven into my identity. It was also the
trigger that moved me to find who I was. It didn't cure my insecurities, but it did increase my comfortability and confidence
with my height. It was where I felt that I belonged and it was just
the right fit I had been waiting for. What I saw around me influenced how I felt about myself. Being around athletes made me
feel proportionately normal. The more tall guys I met, the more
I eased into accepting my body. Before the Academy, I was the
tall guy, but tallness was more common than it was abnormal.
I was surrounded by athletes who leveraged their physique and
abilities to advance in their sport. My height complex took up
less space, but I was still skinny. My trainers pushed me into the
weight room and made heavy-handed recommendations on my
diet. Their goal (along with mine) was to bulk me up. They'd
say, 'keep eating' as if I wasn't eating enough. Nothing worked.
I ate twice as much as everyone else and doubled my time lift-
ing. I didn't get bigger, but I got stronger.

Over time, I stopped trying to gain weight. Not only did it not
work, but I grew extremely tired of trying to fight my body and
morph it into alignment with standards that I never created, to
begin with. You only get one body, and this is the one I was giv-
en. From now until I leave this earth, this is it. I accepted that
I'm never going to be the swole guy with big muscles. I used

the body I had and learned to become an efficient player. My IQ on-court expanded. I became clever in how I used my body. Taking my brother's advice, shorts started to make frequent appearances. I was starting to come into my own.

Basketball was the shift that propelled me into the task of finding myself and accepting what I found. During this time, I granted myself the right to be me. Being different no longer hurt. It was still a challenge, but one that I was okay living with. I found that my difference is not something that I can overcome. My difference is who I am. Instead of overcoming it, my goal was to work on accepting it. There were times that I struggled, but I learned to keep the pain from becoming mentally disabling. My trigger button was pressed less frequently, and the energy I spent thinking about what others thought, I gratefully gifted back to my being for better use. The process wasn't overnight. I started then, and I continue today. The work is constant. I've always thought of myself to be a simple guy until I began trying to decipher the language only I speak. Foreign at first, but now, I can engage in healthy dialogue. My goal is not to be fluent in myself, nor do I even think it's possible. My aim is to become damn good at being me.

The Work That Made Me

Who are you?

A question often avoided and unanswered for many reasons. For one, if the intent is to answer it with depth, the response is much farther winded than the question. The answer is heavy. Beyond a string of personal identifiers, finding the answer requires courage and honesty. This was one process I didn't take the time to contemplate. Possibly because as simple as it sounded, it was the most difficult question for me to answer. Quite frankly, I didn't know the answer. I knew who I presented to the world - most of us do. He was outgoing, fun, and always ready for a good laugh. That was the me that everyone saw, knew, and loved. That was my shell. Its stellar performance allowed me to hide from that question for many years. What others perceived of me and how I felt were vastly different. I knew the values I held. I was secure in my beliefs. I was aware of my strengths and weaknesses. I was fluent in investing personal resources into making sense of everything external to me and everything external that I offered to the world.

Like myself, many people go through life and develop the identities of everything and everyone else around them. Accurate or not, it is common in how we process the world around us. Naturally, the ability to see others comes much easier than developing the acuity required to see ourselves. The difficulty appreciates when depth is required to go beyond a still image and uncover an accurate and honest self-reflection. As a result, I spent more time analyzing 'them' and 'it' than I did myself. I focused on how people responded to me, and my response to them in return - pleasant or not. What makes you happy? What are your triggers and why? What makes you, you? Looking at ourselves is a challenge that can be met with insecurity and even shame. The results are harder to process when they are our own.

We need to take a step back from studying externalities and focus on getting to know ourselves. This requires us to make ourselves the primary object of study and ask the hard questions: the ones that we avoid and those that may stir emotion. Coming to know oneself is far from easy. In fact, it can be painful and uncomfortable, but it is always necessary. Our understanding of the world will lack depth if we have no understanding of ourselves. Dealing with the complexities of life will be that much harder if our identity is unfounded. To confidently but warmly interact with polarity and difference is representative of how you feel about yourself. I've always believed that superiority is less about ego and more about a lack of self-confidence and self-knowledge. Similarly, the everyday bully on the playground or in the office falsely feeds their own insecurity, lighting doubt in their victims. Those who seem to get a rise off of watching others being torn down are some of the world's most lost individuals. You are your root. We need to be able to handle nuances and interact with idiosyncrasies in ways that don't make others feel bad for being themselves. This can't be done if you don't know who you are.

We are constantly expending energy. Our physical requirements take up much of those resources, but often we forget about the energy needed to fuel our mental processes. When the identity you present to the world isn't authentic, more of your energy is used trying to uphold the version of you that you have selected to project. Pretending to be someone you're not is exhausting. Knowing who you are and living life as that person without shame or doubt is freeing. An unfounded identity robs us of our mental strength. It is disabling and confusing. Those who struggle with this often replace what should be their own core tenets with the values and beliefs of others. The world then becomes responsible for telling you who you are. The world becomes the standard.

As this continues, a person can be left feeling depressed and anxious. Keeping up with standards that are not your own is not sustainable. Moreover, because you have no control over those standards and when they evolve - which they do and quickly - the satisfaction of achieving them is short-lived. Over time, you become less connected to yourself. When I was growing up I spent a lot of time trying to get good at things - BMX racing and basketball. Instead, my primary focus should have been working on getting good at being myself. That's the job we need to drill into our children's brains before we start pushing them to get good at sports or academics. We need to teach how to master being you.

Once you commit to looking inside, you have to prepare yourself to be okay with what you find. Internal clarity comes with self-acceptance. In other words, you can't see (clearly) what you don't want to see. You must acknowledge your personal blinders and then enter with an open and honest lens. Whether you like who you are today, or not, you do need to accept who you are at this moment in order to move forward. You need to establish your baseline. Upfront, the journey will involve breaking down many of the walls you've built and peeling back sensitive layers. As you decode who you are, there is an opportunity to discover your power. We are all made complete. You are enough. Avoid the trap of falling in love with superficial imagery, the magic is always internal - the magic is you. You just need to tap into it.

Getting to know yourself may very well be the most challenging journey you will ever have. It isn't a day or year's worth of work. The process is in perpetuity. As we constantly evolve, our job continues. This is a part of our life's work and is one of the most difficult yet rewarding adventures we will embark on. Taking the time to invest in self-work is the best selfish decision you'll make. Selfishness has always received a negative connotation. And mostly, for good reason. However, its bad reputation has long overshadowed the spectrum on which it exists. We need to put ourselves first in order to effectively and wholeheartedly contribute to our relationships and roles. Most importantly, our relationship with ourselves. Redefining what selfishness looks like, opens the doors for intense self-study. It's an uncomfortable shift but worth every joule of energy. During its course, you will begin to find your value, and what you offer will, in return, become more valuable. You will stop morphing due to different environments and crowds. You become firm in who you are. You will start to make better choices and begin to steer through life's curves with more ease.

The Love That Sustained Me

The path to finding yourself can lead you to places you didn't know you had. There will be surprises and new discoveries. What I found extraordinary was the amount of power I reclaimed. It's now no longer given to others in response to how they affected me. I was in control and so are you. You determine how life affects you, to what degree, and for how long. What you can't control is who you are, the body you have, and what happens to you. Start here. Start with an understanding of what you can and can't control. Life happens to us all and disappointments are inevitable. Your response, grace, and strength are what will sustain you, and love is what will keep you.

Once I figured out how to work alongside my difference, I started to enjoy the uniqueness that my height had to offer. I was differentiating between what served me and what thoughts and behaviors caused me harm. I know I'm different, and I embrace it now. I am tall. I am skinny. I am Black and White. But I am so much more than what I see when I look in the mirror. What I couldn't stand about me were the superficial features I falsely assigned value to. When I took the time to get to know my true self, I liked who I was. And what I wasn't that fond of was exposed as an opportunity for growth. My personal journey to self-love wasn't easy, but it's never meant to be. The process itself will demand that you change your mindset and previous standards. It may require you to move. Not physically, but mentally shift how you process life. Once you dig deeper, you may even have to challenge the values you've internalized and the influences from which they came from.

Individuation is key. Scan yourself and write it down. Include your likes, passions, and tendencies. Expand that list with your social and political beliefs, biases, and values. Intentionally take yourself through the process of realizing your individuality separate from the identities of those around you. If that means you start with surface-level identifiers, so be it. The more you dig, the deeper you will go. As you do so, pay attention to where your mind wanders and your body's physiological response. Use them as cues to detect if there's underlying anxiety or joy that arises. My response to public outings was particularly triggering. I would get tight. My mood would change. All indicators of stress stemmed from my dislike of public scrutiny.

A good look into our past will answer many of our why's. Not only do we need to recognize our past, but we need to make sense of it to understand how it impacts who we are today. It's possible a past event that you feel did not affect you, has evolved as a driver for many of the decisions you currently make. What we're doing here is resolving the unresolved, and the events of your past that have often subconsciously invited themselves to your present. The insight gained from this work is invaluable.

As I worked internally, my external responses and reactions aligned with who I was becoming. Certain things didn't bother me as much. I wasn't as quick to rebut and match someone's level of ignorance. My inner peace was growing and it showed on the outside. The outside seemed to lose some of its cruelty and become not so daunting of a place. At least, that's what it seemed like. But the truth is, the outside didn't change at all. The stares continued and so did the impolite remarks. It was always my understanding that the effect people had on me was more powerful than the effect and control I had on my life. Not true. The environment and the people were the same. They didn't change. I did.

Be Kind To Yourself

Another seemingly simple phrase, but how good are we at doing this? From a young age, we were taught to be nice to others, to treat others well, to look out for one another, and intervene when someone needs help. This lesson in kindness begins and ends with the other. It lacks the fundamental tenet of self-love. We can't expect people to love others if they don't love themselves. We need to be able to master this practice. Everyone's version of self-love is expressed differently, but it all starts within. Get rid of gender, race, and age biases. Do not let that determine what you should or shouldn't do. What fills my cup won't fill yours. Learn to say no and get comfortable asking for what you want. My recommendation is to find what makes you happy, understand why it has that effect (not all things that make us happy are good for us) and then, do more of it.

Growing up, I strongly believe my dad was able to give so much to others because he extended himself the same courtesies. I was amazed at how effortlessly he was able to do pull-ups. He loved swimming and working out, and it showed. He loved himself, inside and out. And that is where his confidence came from. He had the energy to fulfill his intersecting identities because he used his energy wisely. Working, looking after his family, present at every game, and on the sideline at each practice. He was very present and happily available. If he was tired, it never showed. His stories on the job were rarely combative. As a child, I would wake up in the night to see his entire unit in the house, grabbing a cup of coffee, guns tucked into their waist belts, and all. People respected him. But more importantly, they could feel his energy. And he was rooted in love. That is what made him a great father, husband, and police officer. Internally, he was healthy. Externally, he beamed.

Being kind to yourself means you'll have to silence your inner critic - the nagging voice that gives power to destructive, ruminating thoughts. Many of the stereotypes and biases that society harbored about guys that look like me, took up space in my mind. After a while, I didn't need others to tell me my differences were hapless defects. I perfected how to conjure unhealthy beliefs all by myself. We need to reject hateful perspectives and replace them with kindness and love. It is astounding how many negative things we think about ourselves in one day. Challenge yourself to pay attention to your thoughts. Make note of how you think and what you say about yourself. Changing your speech is easy. Changing your mindset takes grit. It is a highly repetitive and constant effort. Every time you catch yourself scowling at a part of your body in the mirror, find something to look at that you love. Every time you replay a lie someone said about you, tell yourself the truth. When you reminisce about painful experiences, remind yourself that you're still here. Be consistent. Otherwise, positivity silenced, gives room for negativity to grow. The objective is to become extremely talented in rebutting your biggest critic - yourself. Work on things you can change. Never shrink. No matter how tall or big or skinny or small you are. Boldly be you, and don't forget to show yourself, love.

PART II.
UNDER THE LIGHTS

CHAPTER 3

Necessary Highs And Lows

A New Normal

The pivot from BMX to basketball was heavy-handed. The work ethic required was a shock to my system. Earlier on, I found it hard to fully commit. At fourteen, I was still running around with my friends and didn't grasp the countless hours I would need to devote to ball. I've always been a hard worker, but when I decided to pursue basketball to the fullest, there was a ripple effect in every aspect of my life. One training session after the next replaced socializing with the boys. If I wasn't with the team, my dad had me doing drills on my own. He would make me jump rope and go to the track to run early in the mornings. Miles. I hated every one of them and cried a few times over. I had no qualms with running on the court, but running without a ball in my hand was God awful! It never grew in appeal. There were parts of my training I enjoyed, and then there were parts that I dreaded. Regardless of my feelings or tears, I did it all. I went above and beyond because I knew I had to do more than most to be exceptional. Average wasn't going to make the cut, and my dad never let me forget that.

In the summer of 2004, I was sixteen years old playing on the National Team against Turkey. I was having a good tournament, to say the least. This particular game was no different, I handled myself well. Both offensively and defensively, I was hitting threes and blocking shots.

My coach approached me after the game and asked, "Do you realize what you just did?"

I stared blankly at him in response.

He described one of the last plays of the game, "You jumped up to block the guy trying to make a shot, he sees you and reverses on the other side of the basket, and you just extended your other arm to make the block."

"Isn't that normal?"

"No, that's not normal."

Normal. It started to lose its merit. The thought of it didn't taste as sweet. The more my uniqueness was appreciated, the less normal I wanted to be. Different is what made me stand out. It caught people's attention. But then again, it always had. The change: I valued my difference beyond anything but a defect. The more I groomed and invested in it, the more I accepted it, and the more of it I wanted. My difference is what made me better. It was the catalyst for actualizing my power. To be gifted, to be the best, means different must run deep in your veins. I had made it my mission to pursue membership with the majority and convinced myself that once accepted, I would be better for it. As I gained insight into who I was and what I had to offer, the majority was no longer good enough. I needed to be as far away from the majority as possible to reach my goals. What makes me stand out was the key to discovering my talent and passion. I wasn't an average basketball player. There was nothing normal about my game. I was different and gladly unique.

As my skill level continued to grow, I attracted more eyes. My name surged in conversations and the media. I was recognized as a top performer in my age group. Some people had great things to say. Others had fair critiques. And last and least, some attributed my success to nothing more than my height. Albeit, my previous experiences taught me well. People will always have something to say, no matter how good you are or how good what you're doing is. By the time I was ready to be drafted, the only thing I was uncertain about was the selection number and the team. I matched up against all of the other big names during workouts and held my own. In my assessment, scanning the room, I was the best big man there. When it was time for draft picks, I went to fourteen workouts with fourteen different teams. Each one consisted of a variety of drills, tests, and measurables to assess my speed, vertical leap, power, and agility (among many others). The scouts and coaches provided promising feedback. Despite not having any hype or big-name college behind me, I was comfortable going into the draft. I had no doubts that I would be selected and expected to be chosen first round.

The day of the NBA Draft hit differently. Reality set in. Everything I worked for was on the line. And the pressure quickly mounted. Despite my confidence going in, my nerves took over. I sat in the stands with my family and agents and waited for my name to be called. With each number, my anxiety was raised. At number nineteen, my agent took a call and when he got off the phone he looked at me. I knew I was next. 20th NBA Draft pick, Charlotte Bobcats followed by my name. I stood up and immediately sunk into my family's arms. That moment meant the world to me, and like always, my family was right there beside me to bask in the joy of another win. In the league, my name was new, and to many unheard of. Even if they didn't know who I was on that day, the first round 20th pick was definitely a statement. Those who didn't know me were going to very soon.

The common financial challenges that arise when someone in your family comes into money was uncommon for us. I had heard several horror stories of money breaking families apart once a member made it pro. Personally, my appreciation and love for mine were renewed. My experience was the complete opposite. My parents never asked for money and when I offered they refused. They weren't in a good position financially and still have a heavy mortgage among other costs. Even though they didn't have it all, they always lived as though they had enough. It was never their goal to have it all. That value was inherited by my siblings and me. To have it all meant there was someone without. We were taught that money and things were never the ultimate goals; family, health, and love came first. My siblings were of the same vein and refused my gestures. I tried to give them a car, they wanted no part of that. We settled on rebuilding the house and as other expenses came up, I was there to assist.

One thing I didn't waste any time on was clothes. I eagerly sourced the stores that sold and made exactly what I needed. Coming from France where the Big And Tall store selection was dismal, I quickly found myself inside Burlington and splurged. In 2008, the NBA introduced a dress code, so I partnered with a company named Elevee to have my suits custom made. Whatever tweaks I requested, they provided. I went from no options to no restrictions. My long-lived conflict with clothes and shoes turned into a passion once I had the means to style myself as I pleased. It so happened that I fell in love with fashion. I made sure that every suit was polished to perfection. Every piece complimented my physique. I sought out sophisticated textures and unique designs. 'Sexy Lex' replaced Alexis, another nickname I acquired later in life, one that I didn't mind.

The Last Visit

In 2010, the year after I was drafted, I played on the National Team during the summer. My dad called me often to check-in, and of course, to coach me all the way from France. No matter how far we were from one another, his presence was strong at every game and practice. I could still hear his voice from the sidelines, and even though he wasn't watching, I pushed myself as if he was. He called one evening and mentioned that he was fighting a little something. 'Nothing to worry about, so we continued our conversation. When I made a trip back home his head was shaved bald. I asked everyone what was going on and they confessed that he was diagnosed with cancer. This was the first time I felt my family dynamic change and I felt like an outsider inside my own home. Everyone had known but me. I spent the entire summer living my life unaffected, ignorant of the fact that my dad was sick. We spoke all the time, and no one said anything. I didn't care for their reasoning. It didn't matter if they thought they were doing me a favor. I was hurt and beyond upset. But mostly, scared.

I had to go back to the US for the NBA Summer League. To date, that was the hardest trip I ever took. I didn't want to leave him. I wanted to be in his corner, just like he had always been in mine. I felt extreme guilt going to play basketball while he was receiving treatment. It didn't feel right. When I made mention of staying, I caught wind of his serious side and received strict directions to go play. He said that he would be fine, and what would make him most happy was to see me living my dream. When I returned to the US, it wasn't the same. I performed well and made an effort to celebrate the new life I had created, but my dad was always top of mind. Over time, his condition worsened. I made another trip back home to see him. He had transferred his care from the hospital to the house so he could be more comfortable. When I arrived at home, my dad - the super active, fit, and full of life guy - was laying in a hospital bed. Just as before, I made my case to stay with him. I wanted to spend as much time with him as I could. My family reassured me that he was doing much better since he came back home, and my dad gave me the same story and directive. He said everything will be fine, nothing will happen, and not to worry. I went back, made it through two practices, and rushed back to my room that afternoon. Before I had the chance to call home, home called me.

I don't remember who made the call. Everything went dark.

Anger consumed me. It took over every emotion my body tried to express. And to this day, I am still very angry. Mostly, with the doctor that treated my father. As I had later found out, my dad initially went to get an assessment completed after he couldn't shake a bad cough. Another trip to the doctor once he started coughing up blood resulted in him being sent back home, again, with no testing. The doctor suggested that his consistent coughing irritated his lungs and throat and was the cause for his hemoptysis. Again, no testing was completed. Once his symptoms became extreme, a third trip finally got him the help that he needed. But, they were too late. I always rehearsed what I would say to the doctor if we ever crossed paths and one of the questions that always stuck out to me was, 'If my dad was your dad, would you have done more?' That's what he needed -more. The first time or the second time. The doctor needed to do more. If I was home, had I known, maybe I could have advocated for him. Pushed for a second opinion. The anger I felt provoked a need for some kind of justice. I pleaded with my mom to file a lawsuit, but she refused. She told me that it wouldn't change anything. The anger then transferred to her. I couldn't understand why she didn't feel the same way I did. I thought it would have helped soothe my frustration. I wanted something to make it better, to make me feel better. Negligence took my dad's life. And I wanted the person responsible to feel at least a fraction of my pain. I couldn't comprehend why God let this happen. In all honesty, I was mad at God too. I wanted an answer to the why. Ten years have passed and the pain is still very raw. My emotions are fresh. And although I have come to understand the way of life, the anger remains.

As a family, we didn't grieve conventionally. We didn't talk about my dad and we still don't. It's as if his death never happened. That seems to be how we're all coping. On the anniversary of his death, I light a candle in my home for the entire day. If I feel like crying I do. If I want to stay in bed I do. Whatever I feel on that day is embraced, and my family is there to support me. My mom had just retired right before dad died, so she was spending a significant amount of time in the house. Everything as it was reminded her of him, a pain too heavy to live with. This pushed her to remodel the entire house, top to bottom. It became increasingly difficult to engage with her. She was hard to talk to and quick to anger. Going through the same emotions ourselves, my siblings and I supported her the best way we could.

Christmas was our time. As a family, it was the holiday we all looked forward to. The first Christmas together after my dad passed was inexplicably hard. It was quiet. Dad wasn't there filling the rooms with his loud voice. He wasn't there to push on mom's nerves until she cracked in laughter. My mom lost her best friend, I lost my hero. Our dynamic changed but we remained close and grew in strength. We have never fully recovered from losing him, nor do I believe we will. The pain is too great to overcome. Time hasn't made it lessen, contrary to the popular saying - at least not yet.

Finding Home Away From Home

Life in the US required some adjustments. I was twenty years old in a new country with a thick French accent. I still stood out, but not in all of the same ways. As a tall young (handsome) and successful Black man, women naturally followed. It was very easy to meet women. But it was extremely difficult to find someone I could trust. I dated, but with caution. I never let anyone get too close, that is until I met Courtney. While I was browsing Facebook I found myself on the page of a woman with whom I shared a mutual friend. She definitely caught my eye. With no hesitation, I reached out. I sent her a friend request and she returned the gesture. Shortly after I received a message from her, complimenting my profile picture. We continued the conversation for about two months. I was playing in Portland, Maine, and she was back in Charlotte, so we never had the opportunity to meet. As time went on the distance strained our brewing relationship and we stopped talking to one another. After acquiring a thumb injury, I returned to Charlotte for surgery and ran into her at a nightclub. The next day she had a flight booked to Atlanta but (conveniently) ended up missing the plane. That change of plans landed us another night together, and I took the opportunity to take her out. We picked up where we left off and she hasn't left my side since.

Early in our relationship, we had challenges, but I attribute them mostly to a lack of maturity. We started young. Many of our arguments were unfounded and pointless. We also became professionals at getting under each other's skin. Once the tension became a distraction on the court, we realized we needed to do better. Neither of us knew what we were doing, but we were committed to sticking it out. We made goals and focused on achieving them. Anytime I had a doubt, Courtney was right there to motivate me. Everything she declared, she spoke into existence. She prayed for me, she boosted my confidence, she was (and still is) my rock. Within five years we married in the courthouse and one year later in 2015, we had a formal ceremony and reception.

Courtney was different from any of the women I had met. For starters, in our infancy, anything beyond a hug was not on the table. She made me wait, a standard none of the women I had dated previously held me to. Beyond the physical, her energy was inexplicably different. It was inviting, warm, and she always came with a smile. Within three weeks of dating, I told her I loved her. Within a month, she had a key to my apartment. I trusted her. She was my sounding board. I felt like I could tell her anything - no matter how unreasonable, silly, or embarrassing. Beyond these words, I can't explain how I knew she was the one, it was simply a feeling. One that was irrefutable and consistent. She made me feel like I was at home. A sentiment that I was never able to recreate in the US on my own. A piece of me that was missing ever since I left France, and even more so since I lost my dad.

God continued to bless me. When our Plan B failed to work, God's plan prevailed. We were pregnant. The news took Courtney by surprise. She was slightly down and extremely nervous. I, on the other hand, was excited. I always knew I wanted children, and I wanted to have my children with Courtney. It was hard for me to contain my emotions during the time she was struggling with accepting the news. I treaded in joy very lightly and what felt like in secret. She eventually grew in love with our new reality and we were back on the same page.

IHOP surfaced as our new eating spot. She craved pancakes relentlessly, and for the first time ever, I started to put on weight (but not the kind I wanted). The pregnancy went without any complications. But our relationship was tested. More specifically, I was tested. The mood swings triggered by fluctuating hormones were nothing short of the depictions I saw on TV. One minute she was fine, the next she was a different person. And I had the nearly impossible task of dancing in between extremes to make sure I was being as supportive as possible. I broke down often and reacted to her emotions resulting in countless arguments. Even though I understood what she was experiencing, at times I found it difficult to control my responses.

My son, Carter, was born in October of 2014. And suddenly, my purpose in life changed. My goals shifted. What I held in high regard was reevaluated and shuffled. Here he came and stretched my heart to bounds I didn't know existed. It was a different kind of love. *Different* continued to surprise me.

Reciprocating The Love

Life pleasantly continued. We leaped over our hurdles and rolled over our bumps. As a family, we mirrored much of what I saw and experienced growing up. It was my goal to ensure my children had a strong foundation and a loving home. My career kept us on our toes and Courtney didn't waiver. Both her and Carter were huge supporters, especially off the court. When I found out that we were expecting our second child, I was just as content as the first time, if not more. We were growing in love, strength, and in number. I was going to begin playing for the French National Team once again, so a temporary move to France was required. Before we left, we made sure Courtney was medically cleared to fly. Once the physician was satisfied, we went on our way. Courtney would be staying in my hometown with my mom for a week while I went to the South of France for Pau for the French National Team.

The next morning I received a call from my mom. Courtney was in the hospital. My mom explained that Courtney yelled for her to come upstairs. She was found lying on the bathroom floor paralyzed in pain. The physician advised that Courtney had an ectopic pregnancy that was causing severe internal bleeding. Immediate surgery was required. My mom's English wasn't very good, nor was Courtney's French. The language barrier, in addition to being in a foreign country, was terrifying. Courtney had to trust that my mother would navigate her treatment options and communicate in her best interest. Despite my mother's assurance that everything was in control, I traveled back to be with Courtney. The words, *it's fine, don't worry*, provoked me to feel the opposite. In fact, they were triggering. I was not going to find comfort in words like I previously did with my father. I needed to be there and see Courtney for myself.

The physician explained that Courtney wouldn't have made it if she had stayed at home any longer. To be clear - thirty minutes would have taken her life. The thought of losing her induced a level of fear that was unbearable. Every thought, every outcome (reasonable or not) ruminated through my mind. Although I was breaking on the inside, I fully understood my responsibility to stand strong. Courtney took the loss very hard. Not only did she lose a child, but the experience was painfully traumatic. She worried that with only one fallopian tube, she would struggle to have more children. She worried about all the things that could go wrong if we were to try again. I did for her what she effortlessly had always done for me, I supported and loved her in every way possible. I spoke against our fears and declared our heart's desires into existence. It was my opportunity to show up for her. And I did that. For so many years I battled with a pain that wasn't visible to others. I knew that mentally and emotionally Courtney was hurting. I noticed from the outside that she was struggling with negative thoughts and feelings on the inside. She didn't have to vocalize it. I knew without seeing her tears, she was crying. I did my best to pay attention to what she wasn't saying because I understood that pain - just like all other feelings - is invisible. This by far was one of our biggest tests to date. And although it ultimately ended in a loss, we gained strength as a unit. My love for Courtney and Carter excelled beyond what I believed was already maxed. I held them tighter. We loved him harder. As a man, I grew dramatically. I learned what it meant to serve. Courtney was my number one priority. Whatever she wanted or needed even before she moved her lips to ask, it was already done. For much of our relationship, Courtney adjusted for me, supported me, moved for me. It was time for me to do the same for her.

There Is No Such Thing As The Right Way

Following the death of my dad. I lost my mom's cousin, grandfather, and great uncle in the same summer. I stopped talking and depression consumed me. I was just traded to Dallas, a move

I wasn't fond of. And in all honesty, the court I had worked so hard to play on, became the place I wanted to be furthest from. As a Black man, the focus on mental health is deficient. There's an expectation to be physically strong and mentally sound. Historically, therapy claimed a solid reputation for attracting the weak. Today, there is more dialogue and recognition in mental wellness, but the pendulum hasn't fully swung over to us. And many of us are silently struggling. When I overcame the perceptions of others, I sought out professional support. It's so important, to be honest about when you need help. Our loved ones, no matter how equipped they may be, cannot be our everything. There are times when you need a friend, a partner, an elder, or a professional. Each one of them contributing a unique and particular value in how they contribute to our lives. My wife, as amazing as she is, was not able to pull me out of my depression alone. And it's an unfair burden for her to carry. I began seeing a mental coach to fight my long-standing battle with clinical depression. This is not a choice that I want hidden. It is a decision that needs to be acknowledged. I want others to know - especially other Black men - that it is normal to struggle, and it is okay to get help. This chapter in my life is filled with loss. For me, the grieving continues today. I have found much peace in counseling, and I would not have been able to effectively cope without that support.

Do it the right way. Go the right way. Feel, act and respond the right way.

Focus less on doing it the *right* way and more on doing it the way that makes you happy, that brings you peace, and that's aligned with your values. There is no right way to grieve. Everyone's tolerance levels differ - the ability to handle pain is unique. What life has taught me is that when it comes to pathways and processes, there's no singular way. Your mistakes, hiccups, and detours are all orchestrated to bring you to the place you're meant to be. Your losses, wins, and victories all work together to mold you into who you're supposed to be. Nothing you feel, or have experienced is in vain. It will all be used. Each as an ingredient to fulfill your perfectly imperfect destiny.

CHAPTER 4

Both Sides Of The Ball

An Athlete's Greatest Fear

We've all seen injuries take players out for games, an entire season, and sometimes permanently - destroying careers prematurely. As an athlete, it was always a thought in the back of my mind. Nothing that paralyzed me or impacted my performance, but always a thought. I have seen my peers affected by injuries big and small. I have also witnessed the pressure that outside places put on athletes to recover quickly - often based on unrealistic standards. Despite our heroic display, athletes are humans too. We break down and require time to heal up, especially when our jobs are so physically demanding.

An injury presents a wide range of doubt and uncertainty. The world is watching and opinions are fluent. The nerves instantly kick in and the questions begin to roll.

'Will I be able to get back to the game?'

'What if I return and reinjure?'

'Will I be able to return and compete at a high level?'

'Who is going to take my spot?'

That pressure is grinding. Whether the outcomes are realistic or not, you go through each one. They have the power to dismantle your confidence and get in your head. If you let it, the chances of returning as the player you once were or better, are slim. Injuries are not only physically impactful. You have to realize the mental endurance that's required to overcome the obstacles they present.

Like many athletes, I haven't been immune to injuries and their toll. Unfortunately, I had stressed over the questions above anything more. My first encounter was during my rookie season in 2009. I spent some time playing in the Development League and was doing very well. I had a triple-double, I was producing and hoping for a call back up to The Bobcats, but the call never came. Once I had settled with that reality, I set my eyes on the all-star game that I was selected to play center for. Two weeks before the game, I tore two ligaments in my right thumb - my shooting hand. I couldn't even hold the ball. I was so nervous about losing my ability to shoot, especially after coming off such a high season. The recovery process involved a cast and lots of legs and cardio. My right hand was useless, so I worked on bettering every other part of my body. I even practiced shooting with my left hand. After several bouts of rehab, I was back.

My second major injury occurred years later, in 2017, when I was playing for the New Orleans Pelicans. All summer, I trained, and with every practice, my knees bothered me more and more. At first, I decided to slow down. Instead of practicing every day with the team, I trained with them a few times a week. Mid-way through, I couldn't bear the pain. My knees were killing me. I was at a point where walking was impossible. Knee pain wasn't anything new. When I was thirteen, I was growing so fast that I developed tendonitis in both knees. Back then, it was a pain that was manageable and didn't stop my game. In fact, I declined surgery then because I didn't want it to impact my chances of getting into the league. That summer with the Pelicans was different - the pain became unbearable. I started with two rounds of injections, trusting the recommendation from the New Orleans physician and hoping for results that would offer the least amount of downtime. Each injection kept me off the court for weeks. And the pain didn't subside. After missing an entire training camp, I had had enough.

With a couple of medical opinions under my belt, I left New Orleans to go to Chicago to see a physician who suggested surgery. He claimed that it was the only treatment option that would bring me relief and get me back on the court. I tried to avoid surgery at all costs, understanding the requirements of recovery. My efforts failed and surgery became my only option. They began with my right knee, one at a time (despite my asking to get them both done together). The hope was that I would be able to get back on the court with rehab and my other knee would be kind and improve. But, that wasn't the case. My left knee didn't give me a break. As soon as I healed up, I had to go right back under to have the left worked on. Another four to six month recovery period. And with that, the entire season was missed.

With any injury, doubt is inevitable. You start to question things - everything. All that I worked for, every sacrifice that

I made was on the line and outside of my control. When you're out a week or two, it's still discomforting but hope is present. When you confirm that it is a long injury, your entire outlook changes. I was definitely down on myself. As an athlete, there are never any guarantees. I can't take disability and walk back into the job when I feel better. If I can't perform well enough or if someone grows to outperform me while I'm away, that's it!

The longer you're away from the sport, the harder it is to get back to it. My knee injuries were the longest period of time that I was out of the game. Players that weren't getting time on account of my presence, were playing. They were growing in skill and I was sitting. I watched in frustration. The possibility of them taking my spot became louder by the day. And I couldn't blame them, because I would take the opportunity to shine and move up if I were them too. It just sucked being on the other side. The pressures of athletes to return and fast (and better than before) didn't help either. I felt like I was racing against time. The bar is set so high it seems to ignore the fact that athletes' bodies are human, just like everyone else's.

Beyond my frustration was motivation. I knew it was going to be a fight to reclaim my position and get my spot back. To date, I haven't gotten the chance to go back to a high level of ball. And yes, it is still frustrating. I look at who's on the court, and I know I can produce so much more. I know I deserve to be there. As always, even when I doubt myself, my family has been there to correct my outlook. They have been cheering me on as if I was on the court.

My kids always ask, "Dad when are you going to work out, when are you going to play basketball again?"

To date, they continue to check on me, push me, and keep me accountable to my goals. Those two are my inspiration.

The Missing Team Member

As a professional athlete, 80% of the game is mental. Only 20% is skill. You can be the best, but if you are mentally weak, you won't last (even if you make it). The physical aspects of injuries are impactful, but the psychological impacts often have larger consequences. One of the most important members of my team, while I was recovering, was my mental health coach. The loss of family members in addition to my injuries was mentally exhausting. I would meet with him in person and sometimes over the phone once a week. We would spend a lot of time finding the root of my anger and anxiety. Then we would analyze whether or not the impacts of the feelings were worthy of my energy.

He would always ask, "Is it worth it?"

Is it worth my time, my progress, my hard work, what I was trying to build? My ability to control my emotions and what I obsessed over sharpened. I came to understand feelings of fear and frustration are normal. But how I react, how long I sit in my feelings, whether or not I let my feelings impact my progress, is well within my control.

Another issue we worked on was repairing my confidence and managing the fears I had about returning to the game. All of the negative emotions I was dwelling on impacted my recovery.

Once I focused on what I had control over, and not what I was afraid of happening, it was easier to get through the days. Not only did I want to regain my physical strength, but I also put in the work to become mentally strong - and I honestly don't think I would have ever recovered without the latter.

As men, we are expected to be capable. As I grew into a man, I realized that I didn't have all the answers, and many times I fell short of this standard. With time, I understood that being human and understanding my flaws didn't make me any less of a man. The fact that I acknowledged that I needed help made me a better man, a stronger man. After two years with Charlotte, I was traded to Dallas in 2010. This came as another blow because I had wanted to keep the life I had built. I loved Charlotte. I remember crying about it. I never felt like the Bobcats believed in me and whether or not it was the case, I felt betrayed. Despite my reluctance to go, Dallas was one of the only teams that had a professional counselor. And I used the heck out of him. I strongly believe that every team should have access to a professional psychologist or counselor and promote mental health within the organization.

My dad was my go-to before he passed away. After realizing I needed more than what I could offer myself, my mental health coach and family were there to see me through. But most importantly, I was willing. I was the key ingredient in my recovery and growth. Not only did I have to show up, but I needed to honestly and actively participate in the process. Even with the best advice and tools, the onus fell in my lap. Often, I feel we confuse motivation and inspiration. Inspiration can be extrinsic.

My inspiration comes from my kids. Motivation, on the other hand, should be intrinsic. The desire to change and press onwards needs to be authentic to be sustainable and successful. While the two overlap and deeply complement each other, my experience changed once I was the motivator.

When you view your goal as bigger (more valuable, more important) than the obstacles in front of you, you hustle differently. Motivation is heavily driven by outcome. *What will I get if I do this?* In those instances where you are struggling to find your motivation, carefully consider if the goal is as important to you as you claim. Reevaluate your *why*. And because our needs change, sometimes without our knowledge, ensure that you still want it. When I wasn't motivated to go to rehab, exercise, or practice I placed a lot of weight on my end goal. I was frustrated but I wasn't done with basketball. My energy changed when I became my own head coach. I actively changed my way of thinking and pushed out anything that was less than positive. Talking to myself became the norm. *Just ten left, okay five more, two more.* Athletes are so accustomed to having people push and cheer them on. There is always a large audience and bigger applause. When I was off the court, I was left to my own devices, my own voice. It was a test to see if I wanted it as bad as I did and if it was as important when no one else was watching.

One of the biggest misconceptions people have about professional athletes is that the money we make is a widespread solution to life's problems. Well, we hear it all the time, but let me affirm once again, money doesn't solve every problem. In fact, once you have it, more problems sneak under your radar. Many of life's hardships cannot be solved with paper. Sometimes life happens and no matter who you are or what you have, it's not in your control. Money is far from everything.

Time is another facet of life that can't be bought. I love basketball, but it has also been the reason I have missed many of life's moments. Moments that I will never get back. When my dad was sick, I was too busy to notice or help him get the support he needed. When he passed, I had one week to attend the funeral and get back on the court. There was no time to grieve. There was no time off.

With little or no support from the organization, many players suffer from their mental health silently. From family problems to loss, it's hard to move forward when you can't physically be where you are needed. When that stress weighs heavy enough, it begins to transfer on to the court. If you don't produce, you get benched, others get an opportunity and you don't get the next contract. For an athlete to be at their best, 100%, their minds have to be in the right place. My wife and I learned the hard way when we would let our relationship interfere with my game. Distractions lead to injuries and poor performance. We were able to learn the art of compartmentalization and set strict boundaries that were respectful of appropriate timing.

Be Your Own Head Coach

My wife taught me well, "Speak it into existence."

I believe the tongue can be a powerful weapon. It can also be the catalyst to achieve the desires of our hearts. Say what you want. Declare aloud what you need. Let the universe hear you. There is authority in your speech! What do you say about yourself? How do you speak about your situation?

Often we are our biggest critics, but also our own enemies. Despite what you see, challenge yourself to say:

I will be okay.
It will be fine.
I will do great.

I spent the last several years curving my tongue, and eventually, I noticed a shift in my mindset. What I spent time and energy thinking about lost most of its negativity. I haven't reached a point where I am a completely positive person, but I don't think that person exists. We all think and sometimes say negative things. My goal was to change how often that happens, how long I stay in that space, and whether or not I will let it impact my attitude and behavior. Although we are not in control of what happens to us, we have all control over how we let the ups and downs of life affect us and to what degree.

It's a mental fight and a very active one: managing your reaction and response while navigating pain and disappointment. Outlets are a helpful additive to this process. To be clear, on their own they won't get the job done (the majority of this work is internal). Personally, I found release in things as simple as playing video games. It was helpful to take a break from everything that was a stressor. I was able to shut my mind off and take the focus away from basketball.

Managing stress as an individual is much different than managing it when in a relationship. It requires that you come to know what stress looks like to your partner and how they respond to it. It also demands that you learn how to support your partner while at the same time being mindful of how your stress impacts them. My wife and I handle stress differently, but we've also learned how to help each other. Courtney gets really bad anxiety attacks. Over time, I was able to pick up on her triggers and become familiar with what was effective in calming her down. We also agreed to begin couples therapy. A truly helpful way to break down our problems and remain mentally strong as a unit. As a man, there are a lot of pressures and stresses that women don't realize. Trying to fit someone's standard and expectations produce a lot of stress that is expressed differently by every man. And because most men are not as vocal as women, it is often dealt with silently. Therapy offers a safe space to vocalize those problems, and as a couple, it is great to have a mediator to ensure that everyone is being heard and respected.

Mental preparedness is another tool that has worked to my advantage. Recognizing your stressors and getting ready to handle them is much better than continuing to go in vulnerable and unguarded. When I was playing, I wasn't getting a lot of time. It was frustrating. Sitting on the bench was painful. Eventually, I stopped focusing on when I wasn't playing and started to focus on the time that I was given. If I was going to play five minutes, I told myself to get five points and two rebounds. Whatever time I received, I made mental goals and pushed my mind and body to accomplish them. Mental preparation is key. Talk to yourself. Write to yourself. Record yourself. Be your own hype man! If you are into routines and structure, put one in place before you take that call or walk into that room. Develop your own rituals. Be your own cheerleader. Get comfortable taking control over the inner dealings of your mind.

The Hard Question - What's Next?

To date, I am still training but differently. The game has changed tremendously, mostly because of the Warriors era when threes were dominant. Now, teams want to play small which is a huge adjustment for big men. Us tall guys are expected to be able to shoot and run faster. My goal is to get back on the court. I'm thirty-two years old, I'm still young and I can still play. In 2019, I settled with the possibility that my opportunity may not be the same. I used to play in the NBA, so the thought of going back to play overseas is a tough pill to digest.

When I think about closing the chapter of basketball, I worry if I will ever find the same passion again. Basketball is all I've known. It's been my only professional love. I struggle with the idea of dropping it. I worry about what's next. Maybe my next move is in sports media and communications. I am passionate about basketball, I'm easy on the eyes, I have a great sense of humor and I love to talk. To be completely honest, I don't know what's next after ball. I do know that I want to own a successful company that can continue to provide for my family for years to come. In setting this goal, my wife and I started a security company - F5 Security & Automation. I have always loved tech and I want to provide tools that can help people improve their daily lives.

Since expressing interest in Venture Capital funds, I found a mentor - Rashan Williams - who owns a company in Atlanta. Every Monday we meet and go through the fundamentals so I can learn more. He's been working with a lot of athletes and people in the entertainment industry to learn how to be successful, not just in their particular world but through different streams. He also places a heavy focus on life after retirement. Still nervous, but I'm taking the steps to make that transition as smooth as possible when it needs to happen. Through this process, I have learned that exit strategies are crucial. We often plan and work so hard to reach our goals but rarely account for the period of transition.

As I embark on this journey of self-discovery, I start to pick up on possibilities that are attractive - things that I can see myself enjoying and doing well. During this period I want to set myself up for other streams of income. I want to diversify my financial opportunities and through that, I hope to find the answer to *what's next*? When I got to the league, there was never any guidance around how to manage your money. They gave it to you, but they never told you how to keep it. When I was drafted in 2008, financial planning was never the focus among many of us.

Thankfully, my mom started getting me into real estate and investments. I bought a few apartment buildings and opened a couple of fitness gyms with my brother and sister in France.

In the last few years, I've been more focused on building capital rather than consuming. I want to be able to find other ways to provide for my family outside of basketball. Today, players going into the league are more educated on how to manage their money. They have been exposed to good and bad examples of poor planning and are starting to think ahead. My advice to young athletes is to educate themselves and find a good mentor. Plan ahead and plan for your exit. Nothing lasts forever.

A New Chapter

Playing center has taught me a lot about perseverance. In that position, most of the guys are tall and strong. They're big guys. I have never been blessed with muscles. I was skinny, I'm still skinny. I had to work my way up to get better and stronger. I refused to get pushed around out there. Physically every player is different, and so, there are natural advantages. Compensating for what I didn't have by playing smarter saved me. That mentality transferred off-court and helped me become mentally stronger as well.

When I was playing, I missed out on a lot of moments with my kids. Constantly being on the road is hard when you have a family. First steps, the first day of school - all missed. My wife carried the home. Now that I'm home more, it's my turn. She has spread her wings and runs a very successful event planning business that requires frequent traveling. The tables have turned and I will say that as much as I love my boys, I understand why she was stressed out being at home… Kids are a lot to handle! But no complaining, right now I feel that I am playing catch up on time that I've missed. We play a lot, I do their homeschooling, help with their homework and at the end of the day, the memories I have built are priceless.

The transition has also been challenging for my wife. She was used to running the home, taking care of the kids, and now she has passed the baton my way. I think she also struggles with seeing me at home and not on the court - more importantly, not doing what I love. This phase I like to call *what's next* is hard on both of us. But we have each other's back. While I consider my options and discover my passions, I know she will be right beside me supporting my every move.

CHAPTER 5

Grounded Purpose To Living Legacy

A Different Kind Of Love

What I know and call 'family' continues to evolve. I am miles away from my mom and siblings in France, but God has blessed me with a beautiful wife and two sons here in Charlotte. I admire the sacrifices my parents made to maintain the environment we had growing up. They weren't perfect, and I'm sure there were times they struggled as individuals and within their relationship, but they always showed up. Showed up with love, kindness, and respect. That is what I want for my kids. That is what I want them to see. Emotions are just as contagious as behaviors. Because of this, I choose to make a conscious effort to be aware of the energy I radiate. Stress travels. So does frustration and sadness. Whether or not you're aware, our children are susceptible to being influenced by our emotional state. We need to be mindful! Healthy environments founded by healthy minds are key to healthy adults.

In 2017, we added one more to the tribe, Caysen. Throughout the pregnancy and after, my relationship with Courtney was noticeably suffering. We agreed on couples therapy and that counselor was the device that kept us afloat. Realizing we needed help and committing to that process has been a consistent tool in our relationship. It hasn't always been good. But our love for each other has always been greater than our egos. Every challenge has added to our foundation. She is incredible inside and out. Anything she touches changes for the better. And that most definitely includes me. She has pushed me into uncomfortable spaces just to facilitate my growth. She has made me open up in conversations that I would never think to have aloud. She challenges my ways and thoughts, constantly moving me to new heights in mind, spirit, and body. I am in awe of her patience and impressed with her intelligence. Just like the night we first met, I get lost in her beauty to this day. God saw it fitting to give her to me and I love Him for that. Abundantly grateful for the woman I call my wife.

More than all the things I can afford to give my family, good memories are so much more important. So I am very intentional about creating moments. One of the largest traditions that I had growing up was Christmas. It was our most celebrated holiday. Those memories will never leave me. Thankfully, I have been able to recreate that tradition. We decorate the entire house - inside and outside, and it looks just as beautiful as it feels. Courtney makes sure that every Christmas we dress up and take a family photo. Even though I doubt that it's possible, each year turns out better than the last.

Carter and Caysen have positioned me to learn more about myself and life. I have found purpose in them. Children are a different love. They are a handful and a blessing. It gives me incredible joy to be their father. Every morning I wake up to kisses. Throughout the day I am tackled with hugs. I would have imagined that they would be mama's boys, but they're all about daddy, and I love every bit of it. Even though they are close in age, they're truly their own person. It's amazing to see their personalities emerge and be so different from one another. Carter is very caring and loving - all about the hugs and kisses. At the same time, he is very independent and knows how to enjoy his own company. Caysen, on the other hand, needs more attention. He's the fighter. The first one to pick a battle and the first one to cry for help. The guy will walk over to his older brother and punch him for no reason at all. But let him get hurt, and he's begging to be carried and consoled. Caysen is the true daddy's boy. His mom will be standing right there and he will walk right past her, arms wide open and straight to dad. Nothing can beat that! The love they give off is an amazing feeling.

Their definition of fun is entirely different from what I remember. Anyone with young children can appreciate how different growing up in today's world is from when we were younger. After my homework was done, we lived outside. We hated staying in. Now, my little ones won't go out unless you tell them to. If they had it their way they would be in front of the TV or video games all day. I've watched every episode of Paw Patrol and I am currently familiarizing myself with Scooby-Doo. Regardless of what we find ourselves doing (inside or outside), there are times when I want it altogether done. No matter how big or simple, I create opportunities for us to bond as a family. Every night we eat dinner together at the dining table as a unit. If we're still good on time after baths, we sneak in a movie or read a book. From taking walks to getting away, time together is always top of mind. I get down to their level and often find myself playing ridiculous games with them, with even more ridiculous rules (that always conveniently change in their favor when I start to win). My goal is to spend as much time with them as I can. I will never get these years back. Losing my dad and not spending his last moments together haunts me every day. I want to be physically present for everyone I love and live each day with intention.

Raise Them Up

I was excited to become a father, but parenthood was new territory. There is no handbook. Although Google has saved me on several occasions, my dad has been my example of fatherhood. He was an amazing father and gave me a solid picture of what family, home, and love look like. He showed me what a healthy marriage is and created a blueprint that I continue to follow. Apart from my Google degree, I did take one class to help me prepare for Carter's delivery. I wanted to know what to expect and what I needed to do or not do to avoid annoying Courtney during labor (most importantly). But like all life experiences, you are never completely ready or prepared. You just kind of figure things out as you go along, hoping and praying for the best outcome.

Together, Courtney and I have very similar parenting styles. Our philosophies around discipline are the same. I haven't had to put whoop any butts - yet. A stern count from one to three usually gets the job done. But many times the things they do are so hilarious, I have to dig deep to control my laughter. My boys know I love them because I tell them and I show them. That is one thing they will never have to question in their lifetime. I also let them know how proud I am of them. As soon as they finish any activity they hurry to show me what they've accomplished and I'm always happy to tell them that they did an amazing job. Even if it's a horse that looks like a cat or a twist and jump that barely leaves the ground, I am there to watch and cheer them on, all to make them feel seen, valued, and heard.

Engaging with the boys and listening to their thought process and reasoning is never dull. Their conversations are pure entertainment. They also have an amazing outlook on life. There is nothing they can't do. Everything is within their reach. When I ask Carter what he wants to be when he grows up, I hear a different line of work every time. Some days he wants to be a basketball player like daddy or a police officer like his granddad. The next day a soccer player, by night a magician. Just like my parents, Courtney and I tell him that he can be whatever he wants to be as long as he masters it and he is happy doing it. We want to give them space to figure it out, figure themselves out, and make their own decisions. I want them to get to know themselves, outside of what we (Courtney and I) or the world wants them to do or be. Finding myself after years of being lost was one of my most difficult hurdles. I don't expect that they'll be free of their own battles, but I'm trying to prompt them to think differently from a young age.

I constantly ask them:

What do you think?
What would make you happy?
Why is this so important to you?

Big questions for such little things, but their answers continue to amaze me. Especially with Carter, I can see where he is starting to think for himself and reason with maturity, even at five-years-old.

My parents encouraged me to do anything I wanted to as long as I did it well. They instantly became my cheerleaders and pushed me to my limit, especially my dad. He made it known that I could always do better, no matter how amazing I did. It used to feel like he was never satisfied. Now, I'm certain his constant pressure drilled in a level of discipline I wouldn't otherwise have. He was never content with me winning, that wasn't good enough. He wanted me to win and outperform myself. My dad let his expectations be known - be your best! His mentality trickled into my mindset and pushed me to master my gift.

I had a choice to make in high school. College or the league. I had the opportunity to go play pro, and I took it. While my parents were supportive of that decision, my mom always preached about having a backup plan. Instead of getting a conventional diploma, she made me change high schools, so I had a trade certification once I graduated. I decided to specialize in electric paneling. It didn't guarantee me life's finest, but it did ensure I had something other than basketball to my name. For them, it wasn't about dictating what I should do. Instead, they focused on supporting my choices and setting me up for success within and outside of my dreams.

My dad was pushy, but it worked. That may not be the case for every child. There is a balance in how much or how hard you can push your children. I believe the achievement of that balance is directly tied to who your child is - their unique personality and characteristics. One method won't work for all. Carter responds completely differently than Caysen does. As a result, the way I communicate and discipline them is specific to each child. Taking the time to study who your child is, assess what their needs are, what they respond positively to, are all indicators of how you should parent. Many times, we parent the other way around. We try to make our children align with our parenting style instead of adapting to the most effective methods based on who we are dealing with.

When do you know that you've pushed too hard? I would say when the outcomes are constantly negative. My dad pushed me with ball, but I was agreeable because I wanted it. I wanted to be the best and I understood what the best required. Sometimes we can't see our potential or greatness. Personally, that's where my dad stepped in. He was a constant reminder and still is. Even though I hated certain aspects of training, my love for basketball was so much bigger than the pains that came from the grind. Sometimes grit needs to be taught or learned, and that's okay. Not everyone is born with unfailing perseverance. I want my kids to develop a love so strong that they will wholeheartedly commit to the future they want to create for themselves - whatever that may be.

My children are growing up in a situation very different from mine. They do not have to question whether my wife and I have the means to provide what they need. There is no hesitation to ask for anything they want. They don't have to watch us struggle to afford to maintain our lifestyle. While that is a blessing, there are certain aspects of their character I do not want to suffer. Every time Carter asks for something, he has to work for it. No freebies at our house! We are not raising kids, we are raising adults. If the mini-fridge needs to be refilled with water, I get Carter to do it and I'll pay him five dollars. I need them to understand that money does not come without hard work and discipline. I want them to get used to giving and serving, not only receiving. They need to become familiar with participating in life, not only benefiting from it.

I remind them how blessed they are and do not forget to mention the responsibilities attached to those blessings. Yes, they enjoy every toy and vacation. But, I put them to work! Not only do I expect them to carry their weight, but I also need them to see me do the same. In training, there are days when I feel like I am running out of steam, and they hold me accountable for the goals I have set. As I'm navigating this new space and contemplating my next steps, I want to role model perseverance and dedication even when the desired target shifts. My goal is to help them discover what they love, encourage them, support them, and push them to be their best.

I grew up in a very open family. Our household was encouraged to discuss emotions and feelings so I felt very comfortable expressing myself. I encourage the boys to do the same. Although I was comfortable communicating within my home, I struggled in social settings. For that reason, I pay special attention to how they are developing socially. I need to hear clear communication in terms of what they want and how they feel. We talk through it. I get down to their level and play with them. That way, I can encourage positive and cooperative interactions that hopefully translate when they're with their friends. How they handle conflict is important. The stage is always open to discuss issues they feel are significant and then reflect on how they problem-solve. The subject of bullying is no stranger in our home. We talk about what it is, how to recognize it, and how to respond. My job isn't to give them all the answers. My job is to keep the line of communication open and provide a safe space for them. I want them to become familiar with the self-care and reflection required to develop healthy social skills.

My father treated my mother very well. I don't remember seeing or hearing them go at it much, if at all. After the honeymoon phase with Courtney ended, we argued quite a bit. As we matured as a couple we got better. Once we had Carter, we had to commit to better ways of resolving conflict. There is no grand recipe for parenting. You can do everything the right way and well... you can still run into many challenges. Parenting is a hard job. The title parent signifies authority and control, but the more you do it and the older they become, you realize the less control you have. That is why building respect as a parent is much more effective than trying to parent by control. Life always has its way of reminding us that we don't have any say in how the dice fall. While that is the case, I am giving my kids all of the tools I believe they need to be successful, and more importantly good individuals with high moral standards. I make mistakes, but I am eager and willing to learn how I can be a better role-model and parent for my boys.

The American Dream And The American Reality

"The American Dream."

Growing up, American culture was very influential in France. French people loved the culture, the people, and the country! I remember when we started saying "LOL" long before we even knew what it stood for. It was cool because it was American. From sports to music to fashion, the US dominated from hundreds of miles away. At the time, the dream was to go to the States, get a nice car, a beautiful girl, and make a good living. The key to all of that happiness was money. Guys back then were decked out in gold chains, rings, and watches. All of these material possessions symbolized success. That's how you knew you made it.

When I discovered basketball, Jérôme Moïso set the bar as a West Indian native in the league and opened my eyes to the possibility of actualizing this dream. Once I arrived in America, I saw things differently. My understanding of the American Dream shifted from cars and golds to the grind required to make it from nothing to something. Working your way up to success was the goal. After settling in, my concept of this dream continued to evolve. Once I got married and had kids, my old self would've happily patted myself on the back. Everything that I dreamt of as a youth was my reality. But life became much more complex.

The truth is, for many, the American Dream is more of an aspiration and catchphrase than it is a reality. Black Americans are tasked with learning how to survive in White America. Survive in systems that were created to keep us out and see us fail. There is so much opportunity in the US, but the hate is overwhelming. It suffocates many of the benefits I once held in such high regard.

One of my greatest fears in raising two Black boys is that they fall to the racial violence that is so prevalent here. These thoughts constantly circulate in my mind.

What if they get pulled over?

What if they look too similar to someone else?

What if they become the next hashtag?

Things were much different in France. I never felt racial tension the same way I do here. In America, it's heavy and thick. You can't deny or ignore it. If you can, you are either White or make the choice to live in ignorance. Back home it was more about status. How you dressed and carried yourself was a clear indicator of what part of town you were from and public treatment would vary as a result. In America, no matter who you are or what you have, you're still a Black man - an identity that reels in discrimination, poor treatment, and disrespect. I never paid attention to my race until I came here. Of course, I've heard the tragic stories and read headlines about the consequences of America's racial climate, but sadly, I never truly grasped the gravity of it all until it weighed down on me. Courtney wants to move back to France. She believes living here, in America, involves too much risk and wants to raise them in a safer place.

Credit and capital aren't always enough when you're trying to buy a house in a neighborhood someone doesn't believe you belong in. Status means very little here. Race is always top of mind and a telling factor of how others value your worth. It seems like every week another Black person is gunned down by police, followed by a long plea and fight for justice. Living as a Black man in America is scary. Driving has become anxiety-filled. I frequently survey my surroundings to make sure there are no police around. It's so weird to even think that I've developed that fear because I grew up around the police. They were in my home, my dad was one of them.

My mother is White. My father is Black. The world sees the latter. No matter how nice that car is, how beautiful your wife is, how much money you make - living as a Black man in America presents challenges I would have never dreamed of. I hope that change will continue to dismantle the hate in this country, and we will be able to live without fear of the consequences that arise from having Black skin.

What You Leave Behind

I never contemplated legacy until recently. It was once I started having kids and building a family that I shifted gears. It became more significant than who I was becoming and the process of acquiring possessions. I need to focus on what I want to leave behind, how I want to be remembered, and what I have to give while I am still here. My dad's legacy is so powerful. Friends and acquaintances still find ways to reach me, reminding me of how amazing he was. Neither of my boys had the chance to meet him. But I tell them so many stories that they feel connected to him. Carter tells us how much he misses him and wishes that he was here. When we were moving, we had to take down a painting we had done of him. Carter cried when it went down and reminded us every day to put it back up. My dad's legacy is very much alive.

I want to be remembered for more than the things I've left behind. Money and assets come and go. Just like my dad, I want to be known as a great man, kind and loving, fun, and full of jokes. I want my kids to use me as their model for how they treat their wives. I want them to see how a man takes care of his family and home. I want them to see how I handle conflict, how I tackle my fears and push through my challenges. I want to leave them with all the teachings and examples my dad left me and more.

Giving trumps getting. I know that I am blessed, so my responsibility is great. My boys have a lot, so I expect them to do the same. If they get a toy similar to one they already have, we speak about giving it to another child that may not have one. Yes, we hit walls, but the more I can grow them accustomed to the feeling of giving, the more genuine it will become. They know they are privileged because we constantly remind them. Letting them live in a bubble, unaware of the world outside of it, is a disservice. As Carter gets older, he is coming to understand that everyone doesn't have the luxuries he does and he's appreciative. But more than that, I want him to grow comfortable with being a blessing to others.

I've always had a soft spot for those who are struggling. The constant disposition to protect and help never went away. Serving is in my heart. As a unit, Courtney and I enjoy giving back together, and once the boys are a little older, the entire family will participate. Although Christmas is one of my favorite holidays, for many families it is a reminder of what they don't have. Realizing this, we have done several toy drives in underserved communities to try and make a difference.

When we first moved to New Orleans we could not ignore the devastation around us. At the time, Katrina was ten years behind us, but its effects were very much present. To date, families still haven't been able to recover. So many people were living under bridges and on the streets. Initially, we met them where they were and brought food, water, and other essentials. But we wanted to do more. We wanted to provide support that was more permanent and consistent.

The system is designed to make it extremely difficult to excel when you don't have the means to survive. To apply for a job you need an address. To go for an interview, you need to look clean and presentable. The shelters are packed. Housing is key. Courtney and I founded T.R.U. (Transforming, Restoring and Uplifting) the Home - a non-profit organization to help those who are homeless to get back on their feet and re-introduce them into society. Our goal is to open up more shelters in the area that do more than provide a roof. We want to give people resources and tools that will help them remain successful.

Serving and giving are two life practices that I am very passionate about. Coming into adulthood, there were many ways that I wasn't able to help myself. So I found solace in helping others. That was my outlet. Giving makes me feel good, happy even. As I continue to expand these efforts, I am opening the door to connect with others. Socially developing trust and bonds that I would have never imagined. Through doing so, I have evoked a greater sense of gratitude. God has been so good to my family and me., There's not a day I forget or think otherwise, no matter what is in front of me. I walk and talk differently truly acknowledging and understanding His hand on my life. It puts many things into perspective. I don't react the same way I did several years ago. I respond differently. My attitude has changed. Cultivating gratitude begets personal happiness. Everything I needed to shift into my best self has always been within, and therefore, within reach.

PART III.
POST-GAME

CHAPTER 6

Heating Up

Hidden Blessings

There are challenges that I still bear today living as a 7'2 Black man in America. I still have to duck to fit through doorways and crouch down to accommodate low ceilings. I still have to be aware of my surroundings. I am still a Black man. Always being on the lookout has made me hypersensitive and somewhat anxious in social settings. I would much rather be in the comfort of my own space with family and friends. Crowds are not my thing, and if I can avoid them, I do. But for my family's sake, I often have to suck it up and go with the flow. Despite my preference, I want my kids to benefit from amazing experiences so we spend a lot of time outdoors and traveling. Courtney has picked up on all of the stares that come from standing next to me. It makes her uncomfortable too. She also realizes how it makes me feel and so when available, we opt for private accommodations on trips and vacations. That way we have the privacy and space we need.

To this day people stop and ask me for pictures. I can't confirm whether or not they want a picture with me because I'm tall or because they know who I am. When I have refused pictures in the past, people still sneak them anyway. It drives me nuts! You shouldn't snap a shot of a person that's tall, short, or big (even if you found those games amusing), because you shouldn't want to offend the person. And you definitely shouldn't approach someone and ask to take a picture because of the way they look. The thought of being photographed for nothing other than my tallness doesn't sit well with me. It makes me feel like I'm some kind of animal.

When it's not my height, it's my feet. These size eighteen's are hard to miss, especially since I have such a slim build - it makes them stand out even more. It's crazy what people will come up and ask you, but I hear it all.

Most common, "How big are your feet?"

When I tell them size eighteen, they are shocked as if a man my size is supposed to have smaller ones.

I have found that flipping the question back to them is the most polite way of showing them how impolite their questions sound, "Size eighteen, how much do you weigh?"

Compliments of my brother. He always schooled me on witty comebacks.

Driving has and continues to have its challenges. I remember when I first got my driver's license in France and I was play-ing for my first pro team, they gave me a Twingo to drive - a three-door hatchback, two-seater. It was the smallest car I had ever seen. I gave it a shot, and on day one, my knee hit the gear in the middle of a roundabout. It was minutes before I got out of neutral and by that time I had a pile-up with blowing horns behind me. The next day I went back to the team to ask for a switch and ended up trading with another teammate for a minivan. Not the most attractive, but I fit in it. When I first arrived in the US, I went straight for the Dodge Charger then made my way to a Challenger. Once I got a little more change in my pockets from ball, I was able to squeeze into a Porsche. Of course, my seat was pushed all the way back and all the way down, but it worked. Nonetheless, my options remain few. Most luxury or exotic vehicles won't make the cut (I've tried).

After years of struggling with feeling like the *other*, the consequences have not faded. I realize that feeling different is painful. But now, I understand that I am in control of how I feel. That is something I constantly remind myself - *you are in control of your feelings*. It is my choice, and I choose, every day, to avoid negative thoughts and beliefs. Taking authority over my feelings has been extremely liberating. I have the power to choose what will affect me. Am I always successful in upholding this mindset? No. But, now I know how to fight back. I know where to find the tools to pull myself back up. I am mindful of when I'm slipping back, and I know what works for me because I've spent the time figuring out where my source of strength derives.

What's in your toolkit? My toolkit contains personal outlets, mentoring, counseling, familial support, and self-work. I draw from each of these at varying levels, but together, they serve me well. My recipe will be different than yours. What doesn't change, no matter who you are is that you are responsible for doing the work.

Start by identifying what fills you. In other words, what works for you and what doesn't. What strategies or resources can you employ? What can you pull from? It can be anything from journaling to daily devotions to voice recordings to talking to yourself each morning in the shower or a combination of all these things. You don't have to have a loving family (not all of us do) but you can leverage a relationship with a friend or support group. The goal is to actively engage with yourself. Learn what you need and what is ineffective.

Pay attention to the things you voluntarily do that produce stress and anxiety, then stop participating in those activities. Filter your conversations and purge anything that is not uplifting. I repeat - you have to be willing to do the work. It takes time and grind, but it is worth it. I am so happy I started this journey. Even though I started later in life, it's never too late to begin.

Beyond Skill And Above Talent

Confidence is not an all-encompassing trait. As a youth, I was extremely confident in my athletic ability, but in other areas like appearance, my confidence was nonexistent. Despite how athletically gifted I was, my talents did not help lessen my insecurities. In all honesty, building confidence has been a journey. I'm still on the road to figuring out how to make it a consistent part of my being. Some days, I feel very confident about myself, and about my body; and other days, I have to amp myself up to stay away from negative thoughts and emotions. Since starting this active process of self-reflection, I've realized that confidence is another one of my weak spots. And that's okay, we all have them. It just means that it requires more of my attention. I know very well the effects of not having confidence, but I'm also familiar with how it feels to believe in my abilities. I don't expect to be great at all things, but I do want to focus on building realistic and healthy feelings about myself in all areas of my life.

Confidence can survive without the backing of skill and talent. They sure help build confidence, but they do not always coexist. I've met so many talented individuals who lack confidence in themselves. At the same time, I've also encountered many others who are confident but don't perform accordingly. Confidence is less about what you can do and more about what you believe you can do. The trait is married with many other characteristics that influence perception. If you're a confident individual, people may quickly conclude that you're credible because they believe you're competent and capable. It may put skeptical minds at ease and persuade others to trust that you are skilled enough to handle the job (even if that's not the case). Confidence can get your foot in the door. Professionally, people want to do business with someone that can represent themselves well.

Skills, qualifications, and experience are essential, but they are also common. Knowing how to market yourself is what sets you apart. Not to be confused with arrogance, but too much humility and not enough bragging won't cut it - the competition is too heavy. For those of us who are not comfortable talking about how amazing we are, get comfortable! If you don't show that you believe in your abilities, chances are people won't either. Personally, confidence can make you feel like you can handle some of life's biggest challenges and uncertain circumstances.

It's the magic sauce that can give you the extra boost you need to carry on, to finish, and to succeed. And, it's free.

It's not something we're born with. Some of us pick it up along the way while others struggle to adapt the conviction needed to carry its presence. This means that it is possible to gradually improve confidence levels over time - with intention, it can grow. Successes of any kind - accomplishments, and accolades - can also develop how you feel about your potential. This kind of confidence is called self-efficacy. It means that you believe you are going to be successful despite challenges that may develop. There are other times when success is driven by confidence. Here, individuals leverage their self-belief to push them towards their goals.

Success and confidence have a great relationship, however, failure and loss is an unavoidable part of the equation. Plans change and everyone will experience disappointment. Don't focus on the worst-case scenario, but understand that disappointment and derails are a natural and healthy part of self-growth. That's when our dear friends' courage and perseverance get to shine. That's when we are forced to use creativity and agility. It's all a part of the process. When you adopt that perspective, you spend less time making upsets personal and focusing on the disappointment (the *why me* state). Instead, you have the clarity and energy to determine what you can gain or learn from that particular experience. This is a crucial part of sustaining confidence. Otherwise, it would remain shot every time you miss the mark. Being confident means that you do not let a failed attempt or unplanned circumstance define you or your abilities.

You can separate disappointment from what you know and believe about yourself.

Keep Good Company

My dad always used to tell me, "Don't let anyone see your weakness."

"Why not?"

"Because they will use that against you, try to stay confident no matter what."

That's one of the many things that stuck with me. Earlier on, I took the easier route and focused on looking and sounding confident (which may have been a good first step), but I think I only started to feel confident recently. My mom also reinforced that a lot, especially after my dad passed. She has always been behind me encouraging me to feel good about myself. So, even though right now I'm not on a team, she tells me to keep working, keep going at it. She reassures me that it's all going to work out. Those conversations that I had with my dad, and now with my mom, have helped me get over many humps. Anytime I have doubts, I can call her and they go away. Like many people, sometimes I need another voice of reason to tell me what I already know and believe. For others, it can be a podcast or a sermon. Support can come in all forms.

Most of my close friends have been around for years. What I love about them is that they don't tell me what I want to hear but what I need to hear. Cheerleaders are great to have, but it's also important to have people who aren't afraid and/or have the capacity to stop waving the pom-poms and blow the darn whistle. I can call them and vent, and I can count on them to tell me the real. When I'm wrong for whatever reason in any situation, they tell me I'm wrong. On top of that, there is an expectation that I go and make it right. That accountability is crucial. My friends, Will, Florent, and Jessie, I've known since high school and are back in France. Max and Andrew are on this side of the border. All of them keep me grounded. I know they have my back but more importantly, I know they care enough about me to want to see me grow, even if that means disagreeing with me.

Coming from France to play ball in America was exciting, but I was very nervous. My first practice with the Bobcats was rough. I knew hard work but these guys pushed me to limits I never knew existed. I had a bad habit of not eating breakfast and in true Alexis fashion, I showed up to practice number one on an empty stomach and went right into the toughest drills I had ever done in my life. I started drinking water until the coaches put me on Gatorade, but it was no help. There I was, a rookie from France ready to prove myself, and then boom, there I was, throwing up in center court mid-practice. It was terrible. And something the team never let me forget.

Being a rookie was challenging. You had a lot to prove and a hell of a lot more to learn. I had a great coach, but he was very hard on me, admittedly. I would do something wrong, following after the rest of the team, and he would single me out and go off. Not to mention the language barrier, which posed additional strain. Most of the time I couldn't understand what the coach was saying. Thanks to Boris Diaw (another

Frenchman) I was able to fill in the gaps. He translated a lot, such a huge help.

My wife, my other half, has helped me through some of my lowest points. She has also helped me find my confidence when I had nothing but self-doubt. After three years in the NBA, the lockout happened and I had to go back to France. It was the last year of my contract and I couldn't secure anything. I kept saying that I was done. I had just lost my father, my grandfather, and two family members, and I didn't want to play anymore. Courtney helped me put the pieces of myself back together and get back on my feet. And all she had to do was talk to me. She would tell me to trust myself until I started doing just that. Even with my height, she finds choice words to make me feel good and more secure. That has been an important part of my development. Because of her, I became comfortable accepting compliments - a reminder of the person I know I am. I believe that Courtney has been so successful in supporting me because she has never tried to fix me. She is aware of my weaknesses and ultimately she aims to keep our relationship in a healthy place.

As a parent, it's my responsibility to cultivate the atmosphere for my children to develop confidence. Growing up today is so much harder than it was in my time. Bullying has escalated to new heights and the consequences can be devastating. The kids don't have social media and I don't plan on letting them get an account any time soon. I will hold off as long as possible. Right now, my kids have what I didn't have as a child. They know they are beautiful, they know they are awesome. They have so much confidence in their work.

Parents can become more aware of their child's confidence and self-esteem by getting involved. And a key part of that is making the time to listen to them. I know kids can talk a lot and I know that it can become very overwhelming, but they need that validation. They need to know that you are listening to them and their voice is important. I am tempted to solve every problem for them but I can't. They have to be able to grow to trust their judgment and choices. As boys, they need to know that despite what the world tells them how and who to be, it is perfectly healthy to express emotion and be vulnerable. At the end of the day, I want to make sure they are safe.

Build Yourself Up

As a man, I feel most confident when I get a fresh haircut or a nice pair of shoes. I look in the mirror, just like dad did, and compliment myself. Not in my head, but aloud. Professionally, my career has been a great source of confidence. Making it pro added to that, but it didn't remove all of my insecurities. My most memorable career highlight is the last game I had in New Orleans against the Lakers. I had twenty-eight points and fifteen rebounds.

Today, there's still a lot of noise and tons of criticism. Everybody has something to say. And if they aren't talking, the looks alone speak loud and clear. I doubt that will ever change. During games, I remember hearing fans on the sidelines talking about how skinny my legs were, they would even physically point. The addition of internet trolls doesn't help. Initially, I would jump on the web to read. I wanted to know what people were saying about me. And of course, this was self-harming. I was actively seeking out negativity. Eventually, I caught myself and stopped. Now, any mean or unnecessary comment is met with a swift block. Sometimes we get so used to the negativity that it starts to become our source. That is when we find that we are much more comfortable hearing and being around negativity than we are away from it. It may also get to the point where we actively seek it out. The bottom line, if your source is poisoned, so is your output.

Ideally, confidence and self-esteem go hand in hand and complement each other. But they are not the same thing. While confidence focuses on trusting in your capabilities, self-esteem relies on how you appraise your worth. This in return is a reflection of how you think, feel, and participate in the world around you. Since confidence and self-esteem are such wide-reaching traits, as you can imagine, there are many possible reasons why many people don't have them. Anything from trauma to bullying can affect their growth. A lack of confidence affects performance and self-belief. The good news is that it can be fixed.

But how do we get there?

Work. Self-work to be more specific (yes, I know I'm repeating myself). To change how you think, and act you have to up your mental strength. You have to exercise your mind. You have to build mental muscle. None of this is light work.

I have focused on practical ways to build confidence:

- Paying attention to what I'm thinking.

- ○ Our minds tend to run wild. There are very few moments when it's still and quiet. If you can start to focus on what you spend time thinking about, you will be able to identify negative thought patterns.

- Reframing negative thoughts.

  - ○ This one can be challenging. After you get used to mindful thinking, you can break away from thoughts that do not serve you. Become intentional and picky about what you allow to take up mental space. Are these thoughts rational or irrational? Are they productive? Is thinking about it ten times in one day changing your reality? Even if you are mid-thought, stop and replace it with a positive and uplifting message. What is going well? What do you have? What are you grateful for? What have you overcome? The fact that you have made it this far, to today, reading this material, is a blessing in and of itself! Take the time to celebrate your small successes and wins.

- Filtering my intake.

  - ○ Be careful of what you left in your spirit. From images to media to friends to family to yourself. Get rid of it!

- Getting out of my comfort zone.

  - ○ Find the thing that scares you or that you find difficult - then do more of it. This can be a difficult conversation you have been avoiding or the decision to take up more space at work. Discomfort breeds growth. If you feel that tension, don't run away from it, it has value.

- Make a plan.

  - Make realistic plans for your future that align with your passions and purpose. Do more of what you're good at and more of what you love. It doesn't have to be your main gig, but find ways to incorporate all aspects of you into your lifestyle.

- Challenging myself.

  - Do one thing (towards your goals) a day - at a minimum. Break down your goals (as small as you need), write them down, and check them off. Your confidence will grow as you begin to trust yourself and disprove self-doubt. Get used to starting and finishing what you set out to do.

- Preparing myself for alternative outcomes.

  - Set goals but leave room for deviation. It's okay if things don't go exactly as you've planned.

- Give compliments and receive them well.

  - Struggling to accept and denying compliments is a common sign of low self-esteem. Be mindful of how you react and practice responding in ways that do not dismiss or negate the kind words.

As you start to take the steps to build your confidence, you'll notice that it becomes easier to meet your goals. You'll feel less anxious and doubtful. You'll trust yourself more. You'll feel more attractive all-around. Trust that you are equipped to make this change. If needed, start small and consistently give yourself your time and honest effort. How you think about and value yourself is more important than any opinion or stigma. You are in control. You define you.

CHAPTER 7

Own Your Position

Your Difference Is Your Key

This world has conditioned us to find comfort in categories. It's left us organizing life into standardized boxes to find comfort in the *normal*. The differences that make humanity so beautiful have been stripped to enforce conformity and normalcy. Guilt, shame, and distaste grow for anything that doesn't look or sound like it should. I have been forced to reckon with my differences and have grown to love them, and I challenge others to do the same. I spent too many years focusing on my difference as a burden and feeling it as pain when it was only meant to exist as the opposite. There is great peace in boldly loving every part of yourself, forgetting who thinks you're too this or not enough of that. The further away from internal and outer judgment, the closer you are to happiness.

My losses, grief, and insecurities redirected me to a great place. They were all a part of my plan and play a role in my story. Every circumstance was necessary to mold me into the man I am today. And even though I sometimes wish there were easier ways to learn hard lessons (like reading it in a book or through conversation), I doubt that without lived experience, those lessons would resonate the same. I wouldn't have gained insights or appreciated my present without living through the challenges of my past. It's said that "the best way out is through." I am a strong believer that some things have to happen. Bad things can be repurposed for good. It's all in perspective.

What can you take away from that situation?

What were you supposed to learn?

What is the test? Have you passed it?

In 2011, the NBA was going through a lockout the same time my contract was up, going back overseas to play felt like the end. I had no team and no commitments. I was starting over. Or at least that's what it felt like. I couldn't wrap my head around going backward. I worked so hard but was forced back to a place I believed I was better than. And of course the "why me?" questions flooded my mind daily. But, looking back now, it was exactly what I needed. I had the opportunity to work extensively on my game and get better.

Instead of having fits about what didn't look *normal* to me, I had to learn to trust the process. That situation helped me grow as a man. It forced me into humility and reminded me that I am not above the grind. I am not above any setback. Yes, some things suck, and disappointments are real. But when we shift our minds from pity to understanding, we can discover purpose. We can learn how to take the hits with stride and find value in every moment, even if it is unwelcome.

My wife and I experiencing the miscarriage was another test that was very hard. And although I would love to have my child here with me today, losing him/her helped our relationship. It brought us closer, and we grew in understanding of one another and ourselves. When Courtney grieved by pushing the world away, I learned to pay attention to what she needed. I had to keep up with her emotions, manage mine, and heal at the same time. Most importantly, I will add that it brought us closer to God. From questioning, if we were going to be able to have another baby to now having two boys, we are beyond grateful.

What's yours may not look like everyone else's. It's a simple concept, but when we're on the inside, it can be hard to see and accept. Your package may come in a plain brown box, no ribbons or bows. It may be late or early in comparison to everyone else. There may be detours and rejection that accompanies it. Your path is your path. And from what I've seen and experienced it doesn't matter if it's different. In fact, abnormal paths have the potential to yield extraordinary outcomes. What's important is that it's yours. There's no use in trying to squeeze into a pair of shoes you know are several sizes too small. Do you. Don't worry if it doesn't align with worldly expectations or standards.

Once you discover what's yours - own it and master it. It's well worth celebrating! Too many of us go through life not knowing who we are and what our purpose is. If it looks a little funny or awkward, that's okay. Still, nurture what or who you find. Don't block your blessings because it's not what you expected. Don't let fear and self-hate get in the way of your destiny.

I've fought against things that were meant for me and tried to hold on to things that were never mine to have. My path hasn't been normal. That difference is what brought me to the place I was meant to be - here. When we go against that grain, life continues, but we don't experience life and who we are in that life, to the fullest. It can lead to disappointment and dissatisfaction. And regardless of how much money or notoriety is gained along any ill-gotten journey, anyone who lives a life that is not their own knows the feeling of emptiness all too well. Knowing who you are and what your purpose is, is priceless. Fulfilling accordingly brings peace and happiness that can't be bought.

Even when you are walking in your purpose, learning and growing never stops. Sometimes those lessons come in heavy. Despite everything that's happened and everything that's going on in the world today, I have to find ways to stay motivated and optimistic. The majority of that spirit comes from my faith. I believe that God is always in control, even when it doesn't seem like it. I also believe that doubt is real, no matter how much faith or belief you have. So, my goal has been to learn how to control rational emotions and get rid of irrational ones. Yet another struggle.

I use several tools to stay aligned with that strain of thought. I find enjoyment in the small things like hopping on four-wheelers with my friends or playing a game with the kids. If I stop and look around, no matter how bad things may seem, I am bound to find beauty in something. My kids and wife alone are enough to drown out the chaos around me. That's what keeps me going. Simple exercises such as deep breathing and meditating help me decompress and center myself in the good that can get lost.

Trash The Dead Weight

There is another barrier to happiness - unforgiveness. We hear about it all the time, how it is equivalent to self-poisoning. How damaging it can be to your well-being. How much of a disservice it is. And what we know and hear is right. Unforgiveness affects your heart, mind, and body in ways that are often invisible. It is an opportunist. If you give it access, it takes what you offer and then some, never hesitating or asking for permission. Time and energy are wasted on feelings in the past that the other party may have no knowledge of, and nothing can be changed. When you're bitter or angry you're bitter and angry on your own. Forgiveness is about you. Not about your situation, or the other person. It is a weight that directly impacts your life. Finding it brings you closer to peace.

Despite needing forgiveness from God and others, it isn't a choice I've consistently made with ease. The truth is, there are times I have to fight myself through forgiveness. There's this idea that forgiveness is supposed to be quick and easy. And if it isn't, then there's something wrong with your moral compass. I disagree. My paths to forgiveness have been trying. Sometimes it comes easily, but there are others that I'm still working through to this day. It doesn't always happen overnight because sometimes it's meant to take time. Hurt is real, and it takes time to heal. We can't avoid or disregard our emotions. When our bodies experience harsh impacts, it's hard to focus on anything but the intruder. The human in us is what makes forgiveness a process. And that process - the pathway to forgiveness - has healing properties of its own that we need to grow. While we are on our way, meaning is found and our self-esteem matures. Deciding to let go of anything toxic is a testament to how you value your worth.

To be clear, forgiveness does not mean that you condone the wrongdoing. It means that you have made a choice to no longer let that event keep you in bondage. It is no longer ruminating and top of mind. You are actively letting go of all resentment and anger. And what a heavyweight those feelings can be. I have found that it's difficult to let go of something (good or bad) without knowing what will take its place. If you share the same struggle, begin to force positivity little by little until it drives everything else out.

Our brains will try to trick us into believing that forgiveness is about doing someone else a favor. Constantly remind yourself what forgiveness really is and why it's important. Stop participating in unproductive conversations and thoughts. If you can't form your mouth to say good things, start by not saying negative things or try nothing at all. Finding empathy for those who have caused you pain is a huge step in finding forgiveness. Understand that people can only give you what they have - nothing more and sometimes a whole lot less. Hurt loves to hurt.

Acknowledging your position along that spectrum is important. If you realize you are far from forgiveness, you also understand that you have more work to do. Playing yourself into thinking you have when you haven't is a trap, leaving you to carry the dead weight that you don't know exists. When I look back, I can see the process for what it is. Starting from extreme dislike or even hate, to feeling neutral, all the way to genuinely praying for that person's heart. It takes time. But more than time, it takes work. You have to make the decision to forgive and work towards doing so.

Learning how to love myself required removing all the negativity I allowed to take up space and make a home. During this uprooting, I realized how much anger I had for people whom I gave permission to make me feel small. Years and years of bullying from people I had to see every day and those I didn't know and could only overhear - took its toll. As I unpacked these feelings, it became evident that forgiveness was an area that needed tending to. And when I looked closely, it wasn't them that I hadn't forgiven, it was myself. I was upset that I let myself go, that I wasn't strong enough to stand tall. It was discouraging to realize all the years I had wasted listening to lies I told myself. But at that moment, just like the ones that came before it, I had a choice - to start now or continue to dwell in unproductive feelings. I chose to start. If others are worthy of compassion and empathy, so am I.

Healthy Role-models

There aren't many people I can look up to in a literal sense. But I have many role-models. The list has expanded to include people rarely praised or lifted as such. Black people have had to endure so much and still do. I have realized the extent of that plight living in America and seeing racial injustice and inequality so often. It gives me the strength to witness the resilience of Black Americans. From Barack Obama to every single mother, my role-models are people who stay true to themselves and stand for love. There have been players, like Lebron James who kills it on and off the court. That dude is constantly raising the bar. He's really stepped up as a leader. What he is doing for the culture is amazing.

Closer to home, are my siblings. I'm ten years younger than my brother and eight years younger than my sister, so I've always admired them and wanted to make them proud. I've looked up to my brother for as long as I can remember. In an interview when I'm asked, "Who's your idol?", I say it's my brother Guillaume. He always has been and always will be. I wanted to be just like him when I was younger. He's extremely intelligent and carries himself so well. He warms the room. When he speaks people listen, much like my dad.

I look up to my sister as well. She is strong and powerful, never afraid of a fight. When we were younger she was told that she wasn't good enough for the national BMX team. I remember her being devastated. She grinded for the entire summer. My parents gathered as much money as they could to help her continue training. They got her a ticket to Sydney, Australia, for the world championship. She walked away in the #1 position-destroyed everybody! During those four years, she could have easily given up, but she was relentless. Elodie is strong-willed and never backs down from anything.

My mom is the most incredible woman I know. Clever, smart, and strong. She has accomplished so much. When she decided to be an interpreter she had to learn five languages. After meeting my dad, she rearranged her career just to make it work with him. She ended up in health insurance, a field she had no experience or qualifications in, and worked her way up to the top. That woman knows how to make something from nothing. Her parents grew up during World War II in France. At the time, interracial marriages were looked down on. She pursued what made her happy and that was a Black man - my dad. For her, there were no barriers in love. It took guts and proved that my mom doesn't care about what people think. Her path looked nothing like what the world said it should.

The women in my family are all strong and resilient. My grandmother on my dad's side is no exception. She had ten kids - nine daughters and one boy, my father. Unfortunately, my grandfather was abusive. The day she had enough, she picked up her ten children and left him to start over. I always thought it was remarkably brave, especially back then.

My Advice To You

Study yourself.

Get to know who you are - your likes, needs, desires, and the complexities behind your decisions. And do so honestly.

Forget what people think.

They are always going to have something to say. Someone will always be waiting to criticize. Haters exist at every level.

Fall in love with yourself.

That journey will look different for each of us. But self-love is so important. When you care about yourself, you don't let everything fly. It doesn't mean that you're better than anyone else, but you learn to delete things and people that don't align with your values.

Speak it into existence.

Whatever it is that you need, say it out loud. Get comfortable talking to yourself and letting the universe hear you.

Compliment yourself.

Look at yourself in the mirror, just like my pops, and tell yourself how beautiful and great you are. You have to be your greatest cheerleader.

Never Shrink.

No matter what size you are, the color of your skin, female or male - don't put out your light on account of anyone else. Hold yourself in high regard, and the same energy will be returned.

Put in the work.

Don't forget to exercise your mind and spirit. Self-awareness is an active process.

My Self

What we all have in common beyond being different is that we are all human. Let's remember the next time there is the temptation to focus on what separates us.

After years of living with low self-esteem, I am proud of the progress I've made. My "self" doesn't need to fit. I am in control of creating the space for it to exist, and it is not dependent on anyone's say so. I am not defined by what others see. My job is to be great at being me.

Thankfully, despite life's noise, I have managed to find my way back home.

ABOUT THE AUTHOR

Alexis Ajinça is a professional NBA athlete, who has spent over fourteen years on the court. The Saint-Etienne native decided at twelve years old that basketball was where he wanted to invest his time and energy, leading to a 20th overall pick in the 2008 NBA draft. Now living in North Carolina with his wife Courtney and their two sons, Ajinça has redirected his efforts towards the development of T.R.U. Home, a non-profit organization aimed at providing employment opportunities and shelter for the homeless population. With the basketball season on pause, Ajinça has had the opportunity to grow his business portfolio and most importantly, spend time with his family.

CPSIA information can be obtained
at www.ICGtesting.com
Printed in the USA
LVHW082121291021
701928LV00003B/416